KNIT ONE
SPORT ONE

KNIT ONE
SPORT ONE

JUDY DODSON

a Salamander book

Published by Salamander Books Limited
LONDON • NEW YORK

A SALAMANDER BOOK

Published by Salamander Books Ltd.
52 Bedford Row,
London WC1N 3AF

© Salamander Books Ltd. 1988

ISBN 0 86101 394 8

Distributed in the United Kingdom by
Hodder & Stoughton Services,
PO Box 6, Mill Road,
Dunton Green, Sevenoaks,
Kent TN13 2XX

CREDITS

Editor
Charlotte Mortensson
Designer
Nick Buzzard

Photography
Belinda Banks
Photographic Direction
Lisa Linder
Make-up & Hair
Valerie MacDonald
Stylist
Amanda Cooke

Knitting Charts
Janos Marffy

Colour Reproduction
Magnum Graphics Ltd, England
Filmset
SX Composing Ltd, England
Printed in Belgium
Proost International Book Production, Turnhout

CONTENTS

JUDY DODSON

INTRODUCTION

This book has been a designer's delight.
To be let loose on 24 wonderful subjects, even
though they were designed and knitted in
record time, has been marvellous. It would
have been easy to be over-inventive, but
then the designs may have been unknittable,
and certainly unwearable, which is the last
thing I wanted. I didn't want to end up with a
book of pretty pictures which were just too
complicated to think about. I have included a
few garments to tax those knitters who
delight in coping with a demanding pattern,
but there are several others which knitters with
some experience can tackle.

We all have some sport-mad person
within our families. In my case my husband
is very interested in racing cycling, so that
was one sport that I didn't have to research.
For me it's only walking the dog! And I
couldn't design a sweater for that. Although
some patterns may look complicated, the
fun of seeing the picture emerge is very like
working on a jigsaw puzzle. The fact that my
knitters managed to get them all done in
time was, in part, due to the fact that they
couldn't put them down.

In the past few years knitting has become
a real art form, and it seems there is nothing
that can't be knitted with patience and
enthusiasm. Obviously I haven't been able to
cover all sports. Maybe I couldn't get
inspiration, or perhaps the sport could not be
translated easily into knitting, but I hope
there is something here for every fanatic and
a few 'foot followers' as well.

KNITTING TECHNIQUES

TENSION/GAUGE

Measuring your tension (gauge) before starting to knit your chosen garment is just as important as choosing the design, the yarn and the colours. They are all part and parcel of a professional finished result. Measuring a tension (gauge) square can seem a tedious and unnecessary delay. Once the yarn has been purchased most knitters want to start straight away, but fifteen or twenty minutes spent before commencing will pay dividends later. If your tension (gauge) is too loose, then the garment may 'grow' when worn and washed; and, of course, the most noticeable aspect of this is also that the garment will be too big. Conversely, if your tension (gauge) is too tight, then it will be difficult to knit, the end result will be too small and, as the fibres do not have room to expand during washing, the soap may become trapped and the garment will eventually take on a matted appearance.

Start your tension (gauge) square using the needle size stated in the pattern and cast on the amount of stitches given for 10cm (4in). Work at least 10cm (4in) either in stocking (stockingette) stitch or in the pattern – whatever is stated in the instructions. Press according to the instructions on the yarn label and measure the stitches and the rows very carefully.

If you are getting less stitches and rows than those given, then try again using smaller needles. If you are getting more stitches and rows then try again using larger needles. Different colours can also change a tension (gauge), as the intensity of the dye used can affect the thickness of the yarn, so always use the main colour. Remember that in the future if you decide to knit the same garment again but in a different colourway, then you will need to work out your needle size again.

To show how a difference of half a stitch per 2.5cm (1in) makes overall on the width of a garment I have worked out this example: If the pattern states 22 sts = 10cm (4in) this is equivalent to 5½ sts = 2.5cm (1in). However if you get 24 sts = 10cm (4in) or 6 sts = 2.5cm (1in), and the pattern states there are 120 sts on the back, then the correct measurement would be 55cm (22in) across. With 24 sts to 10cm (4in) the width would be 50cm (20in) – a difference of

NEEDLE SIZES		
UK	Metric	US
14	2mm	0
13	2¼mm	1
—	2½mm	—
12	2¾mm	2
11	3mm	—
10	3¼mm	3
—	3½mm	4
9	3¾mm	5
8	4mm	6
7	4½mm	7
6	5mm	8
5	5½mm	9
4	6mm	10
3	6½mm	10½
2	7mm	—
1	7½mm	—
0	8mm	11

about 10cm (4in) around the whole garment. To measure your tension (gauge) lay your sample square flat without stretching.

MAKING UP/ FINISHING AND CARE

When time and a lot of patience have gone into creating a garment, the worst sin is to hurriedly cobble together all the pieces. I know that knitters often do not like sewing, in which case it is best to give all the pieces to someone who does, because this part of the process is just as important as knitting.

Many knitters 'knit in' the new colours as they go, but often this means that the new colour shows through the background colour on the right side of the work. If this happens then it is better to slip the new colour out, thread a needle with it and insert it into its own colour. If you do not knit in as you go, then weave all ends into your work neatly. The same applies to the loose strands at the ends of row when a new ball has been introduced, so that they do not get in the way when sewing up the seams.

When it comes to pressing the pieces of knitting before sewing up, then blocking is the best way. Blocking means pinning out the garment on a padded board to the size shown on the measurement diagram and then carefully ironing it. But blocking a garment is time consuming and has to be done correctly; so unless

it is a pattern which has pulled inwards, like a heavily cabled sweater, I see no reason for not sewing up first, pressing all the seams and then the whole garment. To my mind this is better than distorting the pieces by not blocking correctly. Every knitter has his or her own method, and each is adamant that theirs is the best.

When joining seams, backstitching the pieces together is the only way when several colours have been joined in at the start of the rows. But backstitching must be done carefully, so that the needle is always inserted the same distance into the work. For single-colour garments or garments which have only one colour at the sides of the work, and especially on shoulder seams where it is best to avoid a bulky seam, taking one side of one stitch from each piece with every stitch gives a firm and almost invisible seam – it is certainly flat.

When sewing in dropped sleeves, i.e. sleeves which are cast (bound) off straight at the top, it is essential that they are sewn into the correct depth on the front and the back. To do this consult the measurement diagram and measure down from the edge of the shoulder seam the correct length on front and back. Mark these points with pins. Take the centre of the sleeve and pin it onto the shoulder seam. Sew the sleeves onto the front and back up to the marker pins.

Looking after your garment is also very important. In general, man-made fibres need washing or cleaning more frequently, as they attract dirt, but a good natural fibre will repel dirt and will need washing or dry-cleaning less. You should always follow the manufacturer's instructions given on the yarn labels, so keep a label in a safe place for reference. If there are no recommendations, then in general use a washing powder or liquid formulated for hand washing. Use warm water (approx 30°C/85°F), make sure any powder used is well dissolved and be sure not to use too much; otherwise it is hard to rinse it out of the fibres. Gently lower the garment into the water and squeeze, always keeping the garment underwater. Give special attention to any parts which may be dirtier than the rest. Do not leave it to soak. Rinse it several times in clean water, being careful to take the weight of the garment as when it is heavy with water it can stretch the fibres. You can then spin dry; DO NOT tumble dry, as the effect of heat on the fibres will shrink and mat your lovely sweater. When all the water has been extracted and if you do not have a spin dryer, roll the garment in towels. Applying some pressure, allow the towels to absorb as much of the moisture as possible, then ease to shape and dry flat away from direct sunlight which affects the colours.

READING CHARTS

Most of the garments in this book feature charts, which, although resembling the photographed garments, have been coloured in using shades which will be easy to follow. If there are any special instructions regarding the charts, these are given before the pattern instructions, but in general this is the method used: Each square represents one stitch and one row. All knit rows (right side) are read from right to left and all purl rows (wrong side) are read from left to right. Always start row 1 on the right, at the line indicating the size you wish to knit, and work along the row, ending on the left at your size line. Start row 2 on the left and purl across to the right.

When using colour, with most of the patterns in this book, it is necessary to wind off small amounts of the contrasting colours and use them only where needed. When another colour is used the remaining colours are dropped at the back of the work. You can buy little bobbins to wind the contrasting colours onto, which makes knitting much easier, as the colours won't get tangled. You can also make bobbins, if you wish, from strong cardboard. Alternatively, you can strand the contrasting colour across the wrong side of the work if you need to use them again within the next 5 or 6 stitches. But the stranded yarn must be kept loose, otherwise the work will be distorted. In either stranding or using small amounts, it is essential to twist the dropped colour around the picked up colour in order to prevent a hole and to keep the work looking even. One way of dealing with two colours at once is to keep the contrasting colour in the left hand and the main colour in the right hand then knit the stitches required, keeping the yarns in each hand. This prevents tangles and knots forming as you work.

On all the charts there are bold shaping lines. These lines denote armhole, neck, shoulder and sleeve shaping. In all cases these shaping lines are simply increasing, decreasing, casting on or casting (binding) off. Always work the last row beneath a heavy line. If the line is over one stitch, then you must either increase or decrease one stitch on the next row. If it is over more than one stitch, either cast on or cast (bind) off the amount of stitches shown.

When shaping the sides of the sleeve, work to the row beneath the first heavy line and on the next row the increase. Continue in this way up the sleeve. If, as in the case of 'Canoeing', there is a heavy line over several stitches, then cast on the appropriate number of stitches.

When working a round neck, work the last row (usually a wrong side row) shown before the heavy line in the centre of the chart. On the next row work up to the first of these centre stitches, turn leaving the remaining stitches on a spare needle and continue on the first side, casting (binding) off the stitches as shown at the beginning of the wrong (binding) side rows. When this side of the front is complete, return to the remaining stitches. With the right side of the work facing, rejoin the yarn and cast (bind) off (unless stated otherwise in the pattern instructions) the centre stitches shown by the line. Continue to the end of the row. Work one more row and follow the shaping indicated on the chart, this time decreasing the stitches at the beginning of the right-side rows. Work the shoulder shaping in the same way by completing the last row before the heavy line – again, it is usually a wrong-side row. On the next row cast (bind) off the amount of stitches indicated and continue to the end of the row. Cast (bind) off the same amount at the beginning of the next row. Continue to follow the chart until the shoulder shaping is completed, then cast off the back neck stitches to give a firm edge for picking up the stitches for the neckband. Sometimes no shoulder shaping is indicated; so when the last chart row has been completed, cast (bind) off straight across all stitches.

YARNS

Each pattern has been designed for the yarn used, and it is important to use the recommended yarn if at all possible. In the case of 100% wool DK, some tensions (gauges) are 22 sts and 28 rows to 10cm (4in) square and some are 24 sts and 30 rows to 10cm (4in) square. So, if you find you have to substitute a different yarn, it is very important to check not only the stitch tension (gauge) but the rows as well. This should be done by knitting a square in the substitute yarn and measuring it, as advised earlier in 'Tension/Gauge'.

I have used natural fibres as far as possible. Only a few yarns featured have some acrylic in them, and in these intensive colour patterns it is essential to have yarns which can be pressed as the work does tend to get a little bit lumpy in places no matter how good the knitter. So a damp cloth and hot iron are needed to block the garment. Also you must remember that the length of yarn in a ball or hank varies from one manufacturer to another. The amounts given at the start of the patterns are for the average knitter using the yarn specified, and if you substitute a different yarn you may have to be prepared to purchase more or less. (See back of book for life-sized photographs of the yarn used for each of the designs.)

ABBREVIATIONS	
alt	alternate
beg	begin(ning)
cm	centimetre(s)
cn	cable needle
cont	continu(e)(ing)
dec	decreas(e)(ing)
foll	follow(s)(ing)
g	gramme(s)
in	inch(es)
inc	increas(e)(ing)
K	knit
oz	ounce(s)
P	purl
patt(s)	pattern(s)
psso	pass slip stitch over
rem	remain(s)(ing)
rep	repeat(s)(ing)
RS	right side(s)
sl	slip
sl st	slip stitch
st(s)	stitch(es)
st st	stocking (stockingette) stitch
tbl	through back of loop(s)
tog	together
WS	wrong side(s)
yd	yard(s)

POLO

MATERIALS

Hayfield *Regal Double Knitting*
50g (1¾oz balls)
3 balls No. 014 (Aran Cream) A
1 ball No. 010 (French Mustard) B
2 balls No. 016 (Tartan) C
1 ball No. 013 (Gunmetal) D
4 balls No. 015 (Spice) E
2 buttons

NEEDLES

1 pair 4mm (US size 6) *or size to obtain
correct tension/gauge*
1 pair 3¼mm (US size 3)
Cable needle

TENSION/GAUGE

23 sts and 29 rows = 10cm (4in)
square measured over st st using
4mm (8 Eng) needles
*Check your tension/gauge before
beginning.*

MEASUREMENTS

One size to fit up to bust:
112cm (44in)
Actual width
across back at underarm:
70cm (27¾in)
Length:
54cm (21½in)
Sleeve seam:
32cm (13in)

BACK

With E and 3¼mm (US size 3) needles, cast on 109 sts.

**Beg lower band as foll:

Rows 1-6 K 6 rows (garter st).

Row 7 (RS) K4, *P3, K4 rep from * to end.

Row 8 K the K sts and P the P sts.

Rows 9 and 10 Rep last 2 rows once more.

Row 11 Slip next 2 sts on to a cn and hold in front, K2, then K2 sts from cn (called C4), *P3, C4, rep from * to end.

Rows 12-15 As rows 8-11.

Row 16 As row 8.

Rows 17-20 Rep rows 7 and 8 twice, inc I st at end of row 20.** 110 sts.

Change to 4mm (US size 6) needles and beg with a K row, work in st st foll chart for back from row 1, using a separate ball or bobbin of yarn for each area of colour, twisting yarns when changing colours to prevent holes, and working incs as indicated until chart row 54 has been completed, so ending with a WS row. 160 sts.

Shape Armholes

Keeping patt correct throughout, shape armholes foll chart*** until chart row 140 has been completed.

Cast (bind) off rem 84 sts.

FRONT

Work as for back to ***, until chart row 110 has been completed, so ending with a WS row.

Shape Neck

Divide for neck on next row as foll:

Row 111 (RS) Dec 1 st at each end of row, work in patt to centre 6 sts, slip centre 6 sts on to a st holder for front neck opening, using separate balls of yarn work in patt to end.

Cont to shape neck and armholes foll chart until row 140 has been completed. Cast (bind) off rem 27 sts (at each side of neck).

SLEEVES

With E and 3¼mm (US size 3) needles, cast on 60 sts.

Work as for back from ** to **, but inc 1 st at each end of row 20. 62 sts.

Change to 4mm (US size 6) needles and beg with a K row, work in st st foll sleeve chart from row 1 and working incs as indicated, until chart row 78 has been completed, so ending with a WS row. 136 sts.

Shape Top of Sleeve

Keeping patt correct, shape top of sleeve foll chart until chart row 138 is complete. Cast (bind) off rem 16 sts.

BACK AND FRONT

BACK AND FRONT

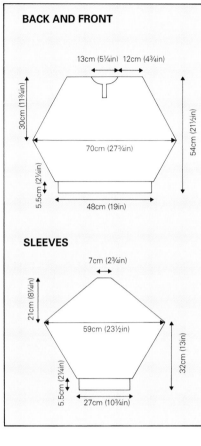

COLLAR

With E and 3¼mm (US size 3) needles, cast on 102 sts.
Work as for back from ** to **, omitting inc at end of row 20.
Work 2 rows more as set.
Cast (bind) off in patt.

BUTTONBAND

With A and 3¼mm (US size 3) needles, cast on 6 sts.
K every row (garter st) until band fits from beg of neck opening to beg of neck shaping. Cast (bind) off.

BUTTONHOLE BAND

Slip 6 sts from st holder at centre front neck opening on to a 3¼mm (US size 3) needle.

With A and 3¼mm (US size 3) needles, work every row K (garter st) until band measures 2.5cm (1in) from neck opening, ending at outer edge.
Beg buttonhole on next row as foll:
Buttonhole row 1 K2, cast (bind) off 2 sts, K to end.
Buttonhole row 2 K, casting on 2 sts over those cast (bound) off in last row.
Complete as for button band, working one more buttonhole 3cm (1¼in) from cast (bind) off.

MAKING UP/ FINISHING

Join shoulder seams. Sew bands on to front. Sew on buttons. Sew cast (bound) off edge of collar around neckline from centre front to centre front (over half of each band). Sew cast (bound) off edge of top of sleeve to the straight part of front and back, then sew sleeves into armholes, matching colours. Sew sleeve and side seams. Press according to the instructions on the yarn label, and keep one label for washing instructions.

SLEEVES

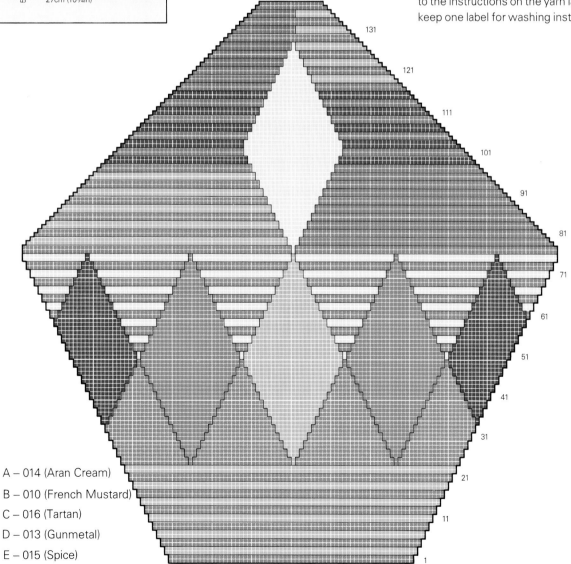

A – 014 (Aran Cream)
B – 010 (French Mustard)
C – 016 (Tartan)
D – 013 (Gunmetal)
E – 015 (Spice)

SWIMMING

MATERIALS

Rowan Yarns *Handknit DK Cotton*
50g (1¾oz) balls
4[5] balls No. 251 (Ecru) A
3 balls No. 260 (Pewter) B
2[3] balls No. 257 (Bathstone) C
12 buttons
Elastic thread

NEEDLES

1 pair 3¼mm (US size 5) *or size to
obtain correct tension/gauge*
1 pair 3¼mm (US size 3)

TENSION/GAUGE

22 sts and 32 rows = 10cm (4in)
square measured over st st using
3¾mm (US size 5) needles
*Check your tension/gauge before
beginning.*

MEASUREMENTS

To fit bust:
86[91]cm (34[36]in)
See measurement diagram for
finished measurements.
*Figures for larger size are
given in square brackets; where there
is only one set of figures,
it applies to both sizes.*

STRIPE PATTERN

Rows 1 and 2 With A, K.
Rows 3-6 With A and beg with a K row (RS), work 4 rows in st st.
Rows 7 and 8 As rows 1 and 2.
Rows 9-20 With C and beg with a K row, work 12 rows in st st.
Rows 21-28 As rows 1-8.
Rows 29-40 With B, as rows 9-20.
Rep rows 1-40 to form stripe patt.

BACK

Back and front are each worked from the crotch upwards.
With B and 3¾mm (US size 5) needles, cast on 12[16] sts.
K 1 row. P 1 row.
Beg with a K row, cont in st st, inc l st at each end of next row and every foll alt row 10 times more. 34[38] sts. (23 rows completed from beg.)
Work 3 rows in st st without shaping.
Cont in st st, inc l st at each end of next row and every foll alt row 4 times more. 44[48] sts. (35 rows completed from beg.)
Cont in st st, * inc 1 st at each end of next 2 rows, work 1 row without shaping*, inc 1 st at each end of next row and foll alt row once, rep from * to * once, inc 1 st at each end of next row and every foll alt row twice, rep from * to * once, so ending with a WS row. 66[70] sts. (52 rows.)
Break off B.
Begin Stripe Pattern
Working in stripe patt as given above, inc 1 st at each end of next row, work 1 row without shaping, inc 1 st at each end of next row and foll alt row once. 72[76] sts. (57 rows.)
Cont in stripe patt, inc 1 st at each end of next 2 rows, work 1 row without shaping, inc 1 st at each end of next row and every foll alt row twice. 82[86] sts. (65 rows.)
Rep from ** to ** once more. 92[96] sts. (73 rows.)
Shape Hips and Waist
Cont in stripe patt throughout, work 9 rows without shaping.
Dec 1 st at each end of next row and every foll 6th row 5 times more. 80[84] sts. (113 rows.)
Work 5 rows without shaping.
Inc 1 st at each end of next row, work 9 rows without shaping, inc 1 st at each end of next row, work 3 rows without shaping. 84[88] sts. (132 rows. 80 rows

have been worked in stripe patt or 2 complete patt repeats.)

Shape Neck Opening

***Divide for neck on next row as foll:

Next row (RS) Work 39[41] sts in patt, slip centre 6 sts and rem sts on to a spare needle.

****Cont on these sts, work 5 rows without shaping.

Inc 1 st at side-seam edge of next row, work 9 rows without shaping, inc 1 st side-seam edge of next row. 41[43] sts. (17 rows completed from beg of neck shaping.)

Work 43 rows without shaping, so ending with a WS row.

Change to 3¼mm (US size 3) needles and with A, K 10 rows (garter st).

Cast (bind) off.****

Return to rem sts on stitch holder and with RS facing, slip first 6 sts on to a smaller stitch holder, rejoin yarn and work in patt across rem sts.

Complete as for first side of neck from **** to ****.

FRONT

With B and 3¾mm (US size 5) needles, cast on 12[16] sts.

Beg with a K row, work 6 rows in st st. Cont in st st *, inc 1 st at each end of next row and foll 4th row, work 1 row without shaping*, rep from * to * once, inc 1 st at each end of next row and foll alt row once, work 3 rows without shaping, inc 1 st at each end of next row, work 1 row without shaping. 26[30] sts. (26 rows completed from beg.)

Break off B.

Begin Stripe Pattern

Working in stripe patt as given above, inc 1 st at each end of next row and every foll alt row twice, inc 1 st at each end of every foll row 13 times. 58[62] sts. (44 rows completed from beg.)

Cont in stripe patt, cast on 3 sts at beg of next 4 rows, then cast on 9 sts at beg of next 2 rows.

88[92] sts. (50 rows.)

Shape Hips and Waist

Cont in stripe patt throughout, work 6 rows without shaping.

Dec 1 st at each end of next row and every foll 6th row 5 times more. 76[80] sts. (87 rows.)

Work 5 rows without shaping.

Inc 1 st at each end of next row, work 9 rows without shaping, inc 1 st at each end of next row, work 3 rows without shaping. 80[84] sts. (106 rows. 80 rows

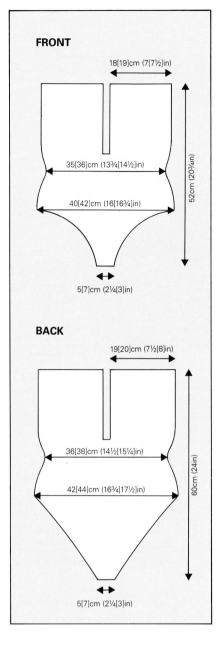

FRONT

18[19]cm (7[7½]in)

35[36]cm (13¾[14½]in)

40[42]cm (16[16¾]in)

52cm (20¾in)

5[7]cm (2¼[3]in)

BACK

19[20]cm (7½[8]in)

36[38]cm (14½[15¼]in)

42[44]cm (16¾[17½]in)

60cm (24in)

5[7]cm (2¼[3]in)

have been worked in stripe patt or 2 complete patt repeats.)

Shape Neck Opening

Work as for back from *** to end, but noting that each side of neck has 2 sts less, i.e. 39[41] sts, after last inc at side-seam edge, instead of 41[43] sts.

STRAPS

With A and 3¼mm (US size 3) needles, cast on 7 sts.

K every row (garter st) until strap measures 2.5cm (1in) from beg.

Work a buttonhole in next row as foll:

Buttonhole row 1 K3, cast (bind) off 1 st, K to end.

Buttonhole row 2 K, casting on 1 st over st cast (bound) off in last row.

K every row until strap measures 46cm (18in) from beg. Make a 2nd buttonhole

in the same way, then K every row until strap measures 2.5cm (1in) from last buttonhole.

Cast (bind) off.

Make a 2nd strap in the same way.

FRONT BUTTONHOLE BAND

With RS facing, slip centre 6 sts from stitch holder on to a 3¼mm (US size 3) needle.

With A and 3¼mm (US size 3) needles, K 4 rows, inc I st at beg of first row and so ending with a RS row. 7 sts.

Work a buttonhole as for strap.

Cont to K every row until band fits to top edge, working 3 more buttonholes evenly spaced so that each is opposite the centre of an A stripe.

Cast (bind) off.

FRONT BUTTON BAND

With A and 3¼mm (US size 3) needles, cast on 7 sts and K every row until button band is same length as buttonhole band.

Cast (bind) off.

BACK BANDS

Work back buttonhole and button bands as for front buttonhole and button bands.

LEG BANDS

Join cast on edges of front and back at crotch.

With A, 3¼mm (US size 3) needles and RS facing, pick up and K58 sts from front along right leg opening and 64 sts from back. 122 sts.

K 1 row.

Cast (bind) off.

Work left leg to match.

MAKING UP/ FINISHING

Sew buttonbands on to left front and right back neck opening edges. Sew buttonhole bands to correspond, catching button band cast-on edge at base. Sew on buttons. Sew side seams. Sew strap buttons on to garter st top in positions suitable for straps to cross back comfortably. Sew elastic thread through the last knit rows on front and back and fasten securely.

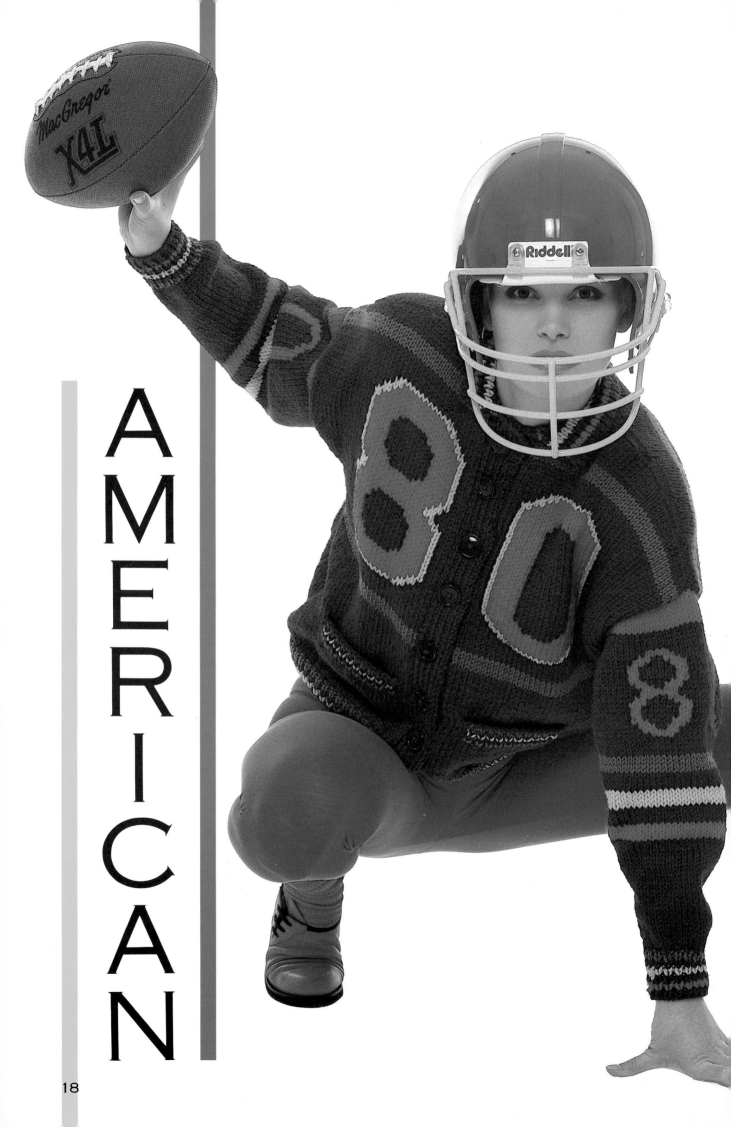

AMERICAN

MATERIALS

Patons *Diploma Chunky*
50g (1¾oz) balls
13[14] balls No. 9703 (Navy) A
2 balls No. 9736 (Yellow) B
2 balls No. 9745 (Avalon) C
3[4] balls No. 9729 (Crimson) D
8 buttons

NEEDLES

1 pair 5½mm (US size 9) *or size to
obtain correct tension/gauge*
1 pair 4½mm (US size 7)

TENSION/GAUGE

16 sts and 20 rows = 10cm (4in)
square measured over st st using
5½mm (US size 9) needles
*Check your tension/gauge before
beginning.*

MEASUREMENTS

To fit bust:
86-96[102-112]cm (34-38[40-44]in)
Actual width across back:
56[63]cm (22½[25]in)
Length:
54[57]cm (21½[22¾]in)
Sleeve length:
40[43]cm (16[17¼]in)
*Figures for larger size are given in
square brackets; where there is only
one set of figures, it applies
to both sizes.*

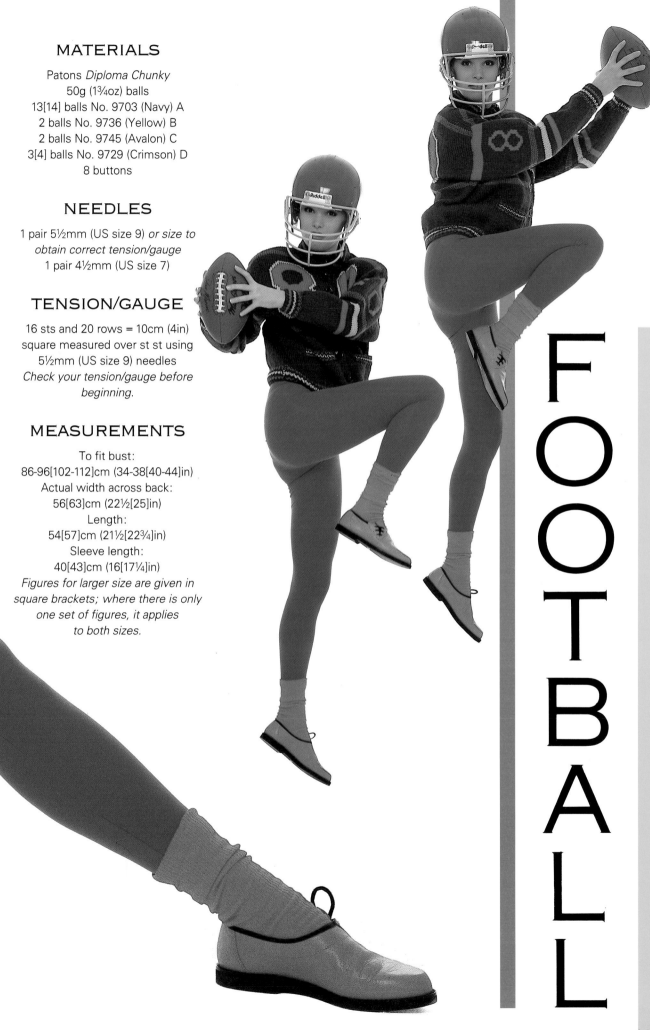

FOOTBALL

BACK

With A and 4½mm (US size 7) needles, cast on 78[88] sts.
**Work 12 rows in K1, P1 rib in stripes as foll:
1 row A, 2 rows D, 2 rows A, 2 rows B, 2 rows A, 2 rows C, 1 row A**, inc 12 sts evenly across last row. 90[100] sts.
Change to 5½mm (US size 9) needles and beg with a K row, work in st st foll chart for back from row 1, using a separate ball or bobbin of yarn for each area of colour and twisting yarns when changing colours to prevent holes, until chart row 98[104] has been completed, so ending with a WS row.

Shape Shoulders

Shape shoulders foll chart. Cast (bind) off rem 20 sts for back neck.

POCKET LININGS

With A and 5½mm (US size 9) needles, cast on 20 sts. Beg with a K row, work 20 rows in st st, so ending with a P row.
Slip sts on to a spare needle.
Make a 2nd lining in the same way.

LEFT FRONT

With A and 4½mm (US size 7) needles, cast on 42[47] sts.
Work as for back from ** to **.
Change to 5½mm (US size 9) needles and beg with a K row, work in st st foll chart between markers for left front from row 1, until chart row 20 has been completed, so ending with a WS row.

Pocket

Place pocket on next row as foll:
Row 21 (RS) K18[23], slip next 20 sts on to a spare needle, K across 20 sts of pocket lining, K to end of left front.
Cont foll chart until chart row 97[101] has been completed, so ending with a RS row.

Shape Neck and Shoulders

Shape neck and shoulders foll chart.

RIGHT FRONT

Work as for left front, but foll chart between markers for right front and placing pocket as foll:
Row 21 (RS) K4, slip next 20 sts on to a spare needle, K across 20 sts of pocket lining, K to end of right front.

SLEEVES

With A and 4½mm (US size 7) needles, cast on 35[45] sts.
Work as for back from ** to **, inc 5[3] sts evenly across last row. 40[48] sts.
Change to 5½mm (US size 9) needles and beg with a K row, work in st st foll sleeve chart from row 7[1] and working incs as indicated, until chart row 76 has been completed. 82[92] sts.
Cast (bind) off.

POCKET TOPS

With RS of front facing, slip 20 sts of pocket opening from spare needle on to a 4½mm (US size 7) needle.
Beg with a WS row, work 5 rows in K1, P1 rib in stripes as foll:
1 row D, 1 row A, 1 row B, 1 row A, 1 row C.
With A, cast (bind) off.
Work 2nd pocket top in the same way.

A – 9703 (Navy)
B – 9736 (Yellow)
C – 9745 (Avalon)
D – 9729 (Crimson)

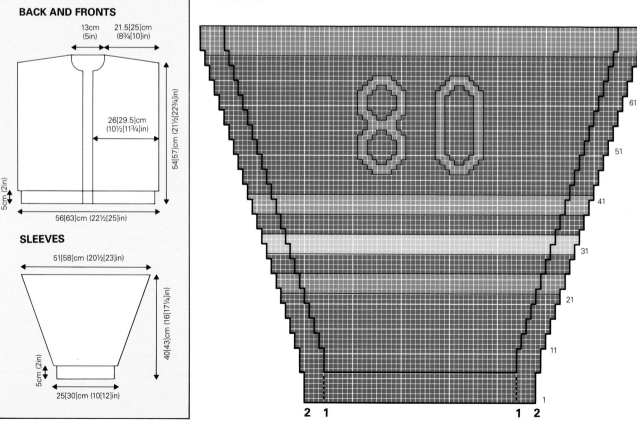

SLEEVES

BUTTON BAND

With A and 4½mm (US size 7) needles, cast on 10 sts.

Work in K1, P1 rib until band, when slightly stretched, fits from lower edge of left front to beg of neck shaping.

Cast (bind) off 5 sts in rib at beg of next row (outer edge) and slip rem 5 sts on to a stitch holder.

BUTTONHOLE BAND

Mark the position of 8 buttons on the button band, the first 2.5cm (1in) from cast on edge, the last 2.5cm (1in) below beg of neck shaping with the rem 6 evenly spaced between.

Work buttonhole band as for button band, working buttonholes to correspond with markers as foll:

Buttonhole row 1 (RS) Rib 4, cast (bind) off 2 sts, rib to end.

Buttonhole row 2 Rib to end, casting on 2 sts over those cast (bound) off in last row.

COLLAR

Join shoulder seams.

With A, 4½mm (US size 7) needles and RS facing, rib across 5 sts of buttonhole band from stitch holder, pick up and K17 sts up right front neck edge, 28 sts from back neck, 17 sts down left front neck edge and rib across 5 sts of button band from stitch holder. 72 sts.

Work 17 rows in K1, P1 rib in stripes as foll:

2 rows A, 2 rows C, 2 rows A, 2 rows B, 2 rows A, 2 rows D, and 5 rows A.

With A, cast (bind) off in rib.

MAKING UP/ FINISHING

Sew down pocket linings to WS of fronts. Sew edges of pocket top to RS of fronts. Sew cast (bound) off edge of sleeves to back and front. Sew sleeve and side seams. Sew on front bands and buttons. Press according to the instructions on the yarn label, omitting all ribbing, and keep one label for washing instructions.

BACK AND FRONTS

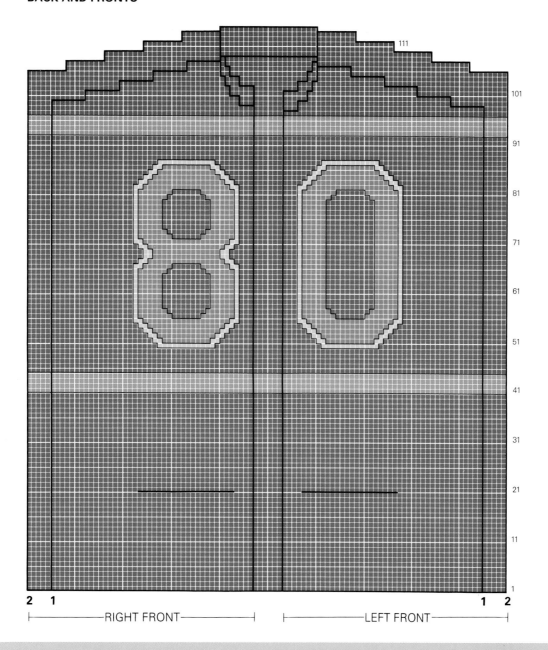

RIGHT FRONT   LEFT FRONT

MATERIALS

Patons *Cotton Supersoft DK*
50g (1¾ oz) balls
7[8:9] balls No. 2284

NEEDLES

1 pair 4mm (US size 6) *or size to obtain*
correct tension/gauge
1 pair 3¼mm (US size 3)
1 pair 3mm (US size 2)
3¼mm (US size 3) and 3mm (US size 2)
circular needles for neckband
Cable needle

TENSION/GAUGE

24 sts and 30 rows = 10cm (4in)
square measured over reverse st st
using 4mm (US size 6) needles
Centre panel measures
18cm (7in) wide
Check your tension/gauge before
beginning.

MEASUREMENTS

To fit bust:
8l [9l:102]cm (32 [36:40]in)
Actual width across back at underarm:
43[48:53]cm (17[19:21]in)
Length:
60cm (24½in)
Figures for larger sizes are given in
square brackets; where
there is only one set of figures, it
applies to all sizes.

TENNIS

on 98[110:122] sts.

Beg moss (seed) st as foll:

Row 1 *K1, P1, rep from * to end.

Row 2 *P1, K1, rep from * to end.

Rep last 2 rows 8 times more, inc 10 sts evenly across last row. 108[120:132] sts.

Change to 4mm (US size 6) needles and beg patt as foll:

Patt row 1 P4[10:16], *K5, P4, K1*, P10, rep from * to * once; work next 40 sts foll chart row 1; ** K1, P4, K5**, P10, rep from ** to ** once, P4[10:16].

Patt row 2 K the K sts and P the P sts except for 40 centre sts, work 40 centre sts foll chart.

Rep last 2 rows 3 times more.

Row 9 P4[10:16], *slip next 5 sts onto a cn and hold in front, K1, P4, then K5 from cn*, P10, rep from * to * once; work next 40 sts foll chart; **slip next 5 sts onto a cn and hold at back, K5, then P4, Kl from cn**, P10, rep from ** to ** once, P4[10:16].

Row 10 As patt row 2.

Row 11 P4[10:16], *Kl, P4, K5*, P10, rep from * to * once; work next 40 sts foll chart; **K5, P4, Kl**, P10, rep from ** to ** once, P4[10:16].

Row 12 As patt row 2.

Rows 13-24 Rep last 2 rows 6 times more.

Row 25 P4[10:16], *slip next 5 sts onto a cn and hold at back, K5, then P4, Kl from cn*, P10, rep from * to * once; work next 40 sts foll chart; **slip next 5 sts onto a cn and hold in front, Kl, P4, then K5 from cn**, P10, rep from ** to ** once, P4[10:16].

Row 26 As patt row 2.

Row 27 As patt row 1.

Rows 28-40 Rep last 2 rows 6 times more, then row 26 again.

Rows 9-40 form patt and are rep throughout.

Cont in patt until chart row 80[80:78] has been completed.

Cont in patt, inc l st at each end of next and every foll alt row 17[15:15] times in all, working inc sts into patt. 142[150:162] sts.

Work in patt without shaping until chart row l46 has been completed, so ending with a WS row.

Shape Neck

Row 147 (RS) Work 66[70:76] sts in patt, turn leaving rem sts on a spare needle.

***Keeping patt correct throughout and sleeve edge straight, cast (bind) off 8 sts at beg of next row (neck edge), cast

HOW TO WORK FROM CHART

Row l (RS) P.

Row 2 K.

Row 3 P.

Row 4 Reading chart from left to right, K all sts except for the shaded areas on chart which are P sts.

Row 5 Reading chart from right to left, P all sts except for the shaded areas which are K sts.

Cont in this way, working all WS rows as for row 4 and all RS rows as for row 5.

BACK

With 3¾mm (US size 3) needles, cast

BACK AND FRONT

24[26:27]cm (9½[10½:10¾]in) 16.5[17:19]cm (6½[6¾:7½]in)

60cm (24½in)

4.5cm (1¾in)

43[48:53]cm (17[19:21]in)

(bind) off at neck edge on every foll alt row: 6 sts once, 4 sts once, 2[4:4] sts once, 1[1:2] sts once, I st 1[2:2] times. 22[25:26] sts decreased in all at neck edge.***
Work without shaping until patt row 162 has been completed, so ending with a WS row.

Shape Shoulder

Cast (bind) off 8[9:10] sts beg next row (sleeve edge) and 9[9:10] sts at beg of every foll alt row 4 times.
Return to sts on spare needle and with RS facing, rejoin yarn and cast (bind) off 10 sts, cont in patt to end of row.
Work 1 row without shaping. Work as for first side of neck from *** to ***.
Work without shaping until patt row 163 has been completed and shape shoulder to match first side.

FRONT

Work as for back.

NECKBAND

Join right shoulder seam.
With 3¼mm (US size 3) circular needle and RS facing, pick up and K 33 sts down left side of front neck, 10 sts from centre, 33 sts up right side of front neck, 33 sts down right side of back neck, 10 sts from centre and 33 sts from up left side of back neck. 152 sts.
Working back and forth in rows, work 8 rows in moss (seed) st as for back.
Change to 3mm (US size 2) circular needle and cont in moss (seed) st until neckband measures 3cm (1¼in).
Cast (bind) off loosely in moss (seed) st.

ARMBANDS

With 3¼mm (US size 3) needles and RS facing, pick up and K76 sts from straight edge of right sleeve.
Work in moss (seed) st for 3cm (1¼in).
Cast (bind) off loosely in moss (seed) st.
Join left shoulder seam and neckband.
Work armband on left sleeve as for right sleeve.

MAKING UP/ FINISHING

Dampen pieces and pin out on a padded surface RS up to correct size foll measurement diagram. Leave to dry. Sew side seams. Keep one yarn label for washing instructions.

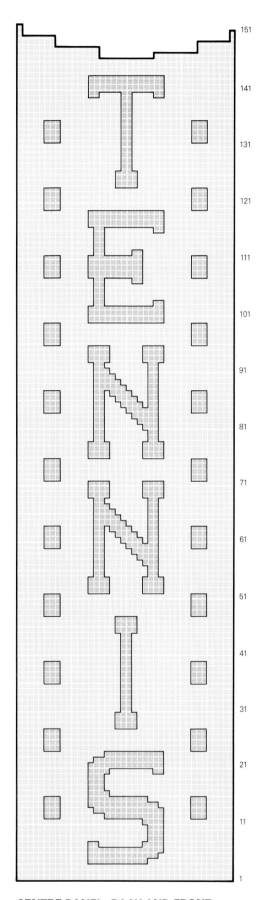

CENTRE PANEL: BACK AND FRONT

P on RS and K on WS   2284 (Cream)

K on RS and P on WS

MATERIALS

Emu *Superwash DK*
50g (1¾oz) balls
4 balls No. 3085 (Light Green) A
3 balls No. 3084 (Dark Green) B
4 balls No. 3023 (Sludge Green) C
1 ball No. 3011 (Dark Brown) D
1 ball No. 3099 (Mid Brown) E
1 ball No. 3098 (Natural) F
1 ball No. 3060 (Royal) G
1 ball No. 3092 (Gold) H
1 ball No. 3002 (Red) I
1 ball No. 3050 (Rust) J
1 ball No. 3017 (Orange) L
3 buttons

NEEDLES

1 pair 4mm (US size 6) *or size to obtain
correct tension/gauge*
1 pair 3¼mm (US size 3)

TENSION/GAUGE

23 sts and 29 rows = 10cm (4in)
square measured over chart patt using
4mm (US size 6) needles
*Check your tension/gauge before
beginning.*

MEASUREMENTS

To fit bust:
86-9l[96-102]cm (34-36[38-40]in)
Actual width across back:
48[53]cm (19[21]in)
Length:
57[58]cm (22¾[23¼]in)
Sleeve length:
49cm (19¾in)
*Figures for larger size are given
in square brackets; where
there is only one set of figures,
it applies to both sizes.*

SHOOTING

BACK

With A and 4mm (US size 6) needles, cast on 110[122] sts.

Beg with a K row, work in st st foll chart for back from row 1, using a separate ball or bobbin of yarn for each area of colour and twisting yarns when changing colours to prevent holes, until chart row 142[144] has been completed, so ending with a WS row.

Shape Shoulders

Keeping patt correct, shape shoulder foll chart.

Cast (bind) off rem 34 sts for back neck.

FRONT

Work as for back, but foll chart for front, until chart 108 has been completed, so ending with a WS row.

Shape Neck

Divide for neck on next row as foll:

Row 109 (RS) Work in patt to centre 6 sts, slip centre 6 sts on to a st holder for front neck opening, using separate balls of yarn work in patt to end.

Cont to shape neck foll chart until chart row 142[144] has been completed, so ending with a WS row.

Shape Shoulders

Complete neck shaping and shape shoulders foll chart.

SLEEVES

With A and 4mm (US size 6) needles, cast on 54[60] sts.

Beg with a K row, work in st st foll sleeve chart from row 1 and working incs as indicated, until chart row 120 has been completed. 108[114] sts.

Cast (bind) off.

BUTTON BAND

With A and 3¼mm (US size 3) needles, cast on 7 sts.

K every row (garter st) until band fits from beg of neck opening to beg of neck shaping, ending at outer edge.

Cast (bind) off first 3 sts, and slip rem 4 sts on to a stitch holder.

BUTTONHOLE BAND

Mark the position of 3 buttons on the button band, the first 2cm (¾in) from cast on edge, the last 1.5cm (½in) from cast (bound) off edge and the rem between these 2.

With RS facing, slip 6 sts from st holder at centre front neck opening on to a 3¼mm (US size 3) needle.

With A and 3¼mm (US size 3) needles, K I row, inc I st at end of row. 7 sts.

Work buttonhole band as for button band, working buttonholes to correspond with markers as foll:

Buttonhole row 1 (RS) K3, cast (bind) off 1 st, K to end.

Buttonhole row 2 K to end, casting on 1 st over st cast (bound) off in last row.

COLLAR

Join shoulder seams.

With 3¼mm (US size 3) needles, A and RS facing, K4 sts of buttonhole band from stitch holder, pick up and K26 sts up right front neck edge, 34 sts from back neck, 26 sts down left front and 4 sts of button band from st holder. 94 sts.

K every row (garter st) for 7.5cm (3in).

Cast (bind) off.

LOWER BACK BAND

With J and 3¼mm (US size 3) needles, cast on 20 sts.

K every row (garter st) in stripes as foll:
* 2 rows J, 2 rows A*, rep from * to * 12

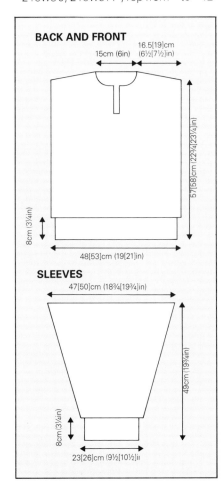

BACK AND FRONT

15cm (6in) 16.5[19]cm (6½[7½]in)

57[58]cm (22¾[23¼]in)

8cm (3¼in)

48[53]cm (19[21]in)

SLEEVES

47[50]cm (18¾[19¾]in)

49cm (19¾in)

8cm (3¼in)

23[26]cm (9½[10½]in)

A – 3085 (Light Green)
B – 3084 (Dark Green)
C – 3023 (Sludge Green)

D – 3011 (Dark Brown)
E – 3099 (Mid Brown)
F – 3098 (Natural)
G – 3060 (Royal)

H – 3092 (Gold)
I – 3002 (Red)
J – 3050 (Rust)
L – 3017 (Orange)

BACK

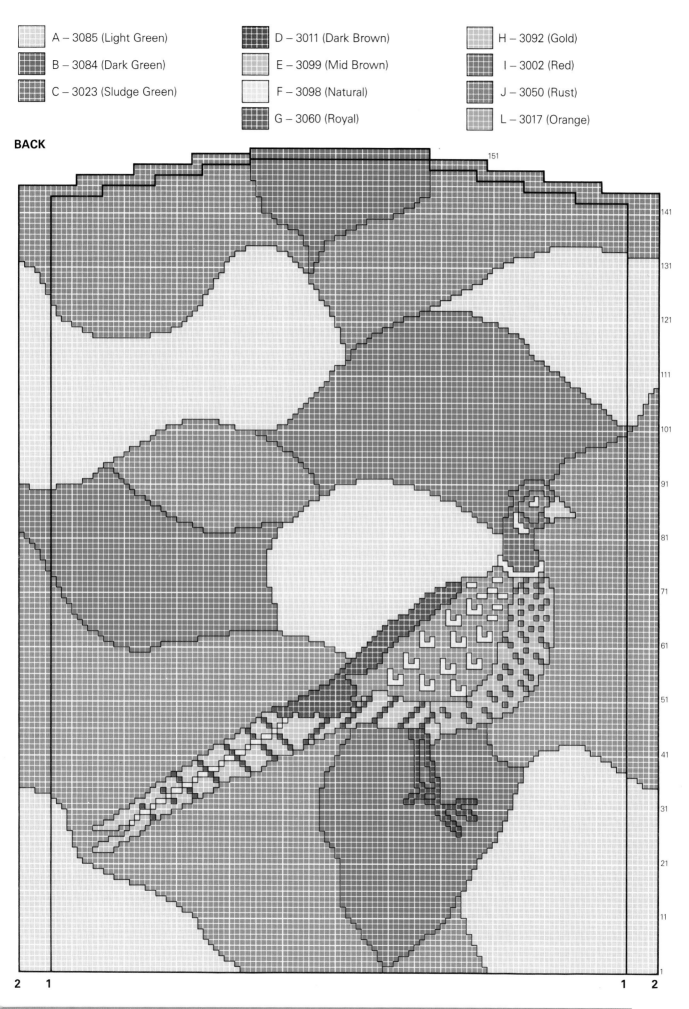

times more, ** 2 rows J, 2 rows C**, rep from ** to ** 20 times more, *** 2 rows J, 2 rows A ***, rep from *** to *** 14 times more, 2 rows J.
With J, cast (bind) off.

LOWER FRONT BAND

With J and 3¼mm (US size 3) needles, cast on 20 sts.
K every row (garter st) in stripes as foll:
2 rows J, 2 rows A, rep from * to * 4 times more, **2 rows J, 2 rows B**, rep from ** to ** 13 times more, ***2 rows J, 2 rows C***, rep from *** to *** 21 times more, ****2 rows J, 2 rows A****, rep from **** to **** 7 times more, 2 rows J.
With J, cast (bind) off.

CUFFS

With J and 3¼mm (US size 3) needles, cast on 20 sts.
K every row (garter st) in stripes as foll:
2 rows J, 2 rows A, rep from * to * 4 times more, **2 rows J, 2 rows C**, rep from ** to ** 4 times more, ***2 rows J, 2 rows A***, rep from *** to *** 12 times more.
With A, cast (bind) off.
Make a 2nd cuff in the same way.

MAKING UP/ FINISHING

Sew lower back band on to cast on edge of back, matching colours. Sew on lower front band and cuffs in the same way. Sew cast (bound) off edge of sleeves to back and front. Sew sleeve and side seams. Sew button and button-hole bands on to front neck opening, catching cast-on edge of button band on WS at centre front. Sew on buttons. Press according to the instructions on the yarn label, omitting all ribbing, and keep one yarn label for washing instructions.

SLEEVES

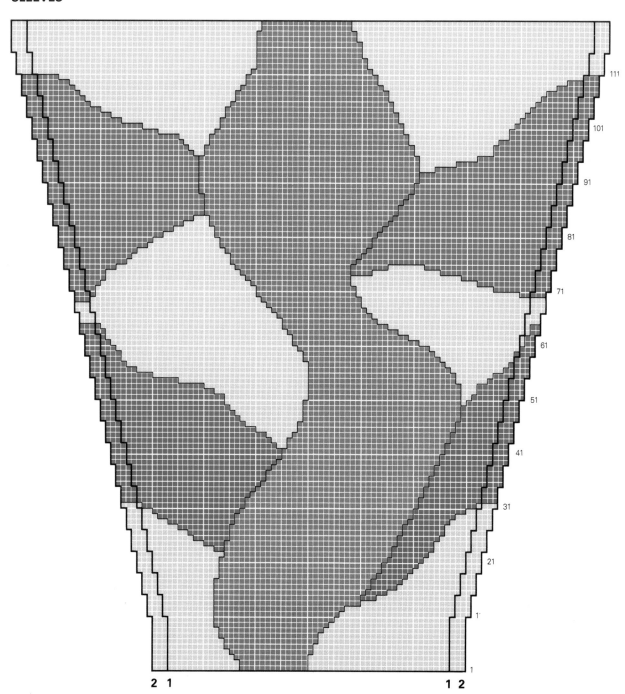

2 1   1 2

FRONT

151

141

131

121

111

101

91

81

71

61

51

41

31

21

11

1

2　　1

1　　2

SKIING

MATERIALS

Wendy *Ascot Chunky*
50g (1¾oz) balls
11 balls No. 401 (Jersey Cream) A
9 balls No. 423 (Jet) B
1 ball No. 399 (Aztec Gold) C
1 ball No. 416 (Rustic Red) D
1 ball No. 411 (Hazelnut) E
4 buttons

NEEDLES

1 pair 5½mm (US size 9) *or size to
obtain correct tension/gauge*
1 pair 4½mm (US size 7)

TENSION/GAUGE

16 sts and 20 rows = 10cm (4in)
square measured over colour patt
using 5½mm (US size 9) needles
*Check your tension/gauge
before beginning.*

MEASUREMENTS

One size to fit up to bust:
107cm (42in)
Actual width across back:
59cm (23¾in)
Length:
69cm (27½in)
Sleeve length:
45cm (18in)

BACK

With A and 4½mm (US size 7) needles, cast on 87 sts.

Work in K1, P1 rib for 9cm (3½in), inc 8 sts evenly across last row. 95 sts.

Change to 5½mm (US size 9) needles and beg with a K row, work in st st foll chart for back from row 1, using a separate ball or bobbin of yarn for each area of colour and twisting yarns when changing colours to prevent holes, until chart row 120 has been completed.

Cast (bind) off in correct colours.

FRONT

Work as for back, but foll chart for front, until chart row 96 has been completed, so ending with a WS row.

Shape Neck

Divide for neck on next row as foll:

Row 97 (RS) Work in patt to centre 5 sts, slip centre 5 sts on to a st holder for front neck opening, using separate balls of yarn, work in patt to end.

Cont to shape neck foll chart until chart row 120 has been completed.

Cast (bind) off rem 33 sts (at each side of neck) in correct colours.

RIGHT SLEEVE

With A and 4½mm (US size 7) needles, cast on 32 sts.

Work in K1, P1 rib for 9cm (3½in), inc 14 sts evenly across last row. 46 sts.

Change to 5½mm (US size 9) needles and beg with a K row, work in st st foll right sleeve chart from row 1 and work-ing incs as indicated, until chart row 72 has been completed. 116 sts.

Cast (bind) off in correct colours.

LEFT SLEEVE

Work as for right sleeve, but foll left sleeve chart.

COLLAR

Join shoulder seams. With A, 4½mm (US size 7) needles and RS facing, pick up and K15 sts up right front neck edge (omitting neck opening), 29 sts from back neck and 15 sts down left front neck edge (omitting neck opening). 59 sts.

Work in K1, P1 rib for 16cm (6in).

Cast (bind) off loosely in rib.

RIGHT FRONT BAND

Slip 5 sts from st holder at centre front neck opening on to a 4½mm (US size 7) needle.

With A and 4½mm (US size 7) needles, work in K1, P1 rib, inc 3 sts evenly across first row, until band measures 2cm (¾in) from neck opening, ending at outside edge. 8 sts.

Beg buttonhole on next row as foll:

Buttonhole row 1 Rib 3, cast (bind) off 2 sts, rib to end.

Buttonhole row 2 Work in rib, casting on 2 sts over 2 sts cast (bound) off in last row.

Cont in rib, work one more buttonhole 4cm (1½in) from base of first. Cont in rib until band fits up neck opening and along side of collar to cast (bound) off edge of collar.

Cast (bind) off loosely in rib.

LEFT FRONT BAND

With A and 4½mm (US size 7) needles, cast on 8 sts.

Work in K1, P1 rib until band measures 16cm (6in) from cast-on edge. Make a buttonhole in the centre, and another buttonhole 4cm (1½in) from base of first. Cont in rib until band fits to cast (bound) off edge of collar.

Cast (bind) off loosely in rib.

MAKING UP/ FINISHING

Join back seam of collar. Sew bands on to front neck opening and edge of collar. Sew on buttons, and fold over collar. Sew cast (bound) off edge of sleeves to back and front, matching checks. Sew sleeve and side seams. Press according to the instructions on the yarn label, omitting all ribbing, and keep one label for washing instructions.

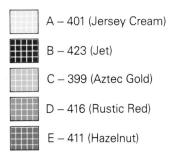

A – 401 (Jersey Cream)
B – 423 (Jet)
C – 399 (Aztec Gold)
D – 416 (Rustic Red)
E – 411 (Hazelnut)

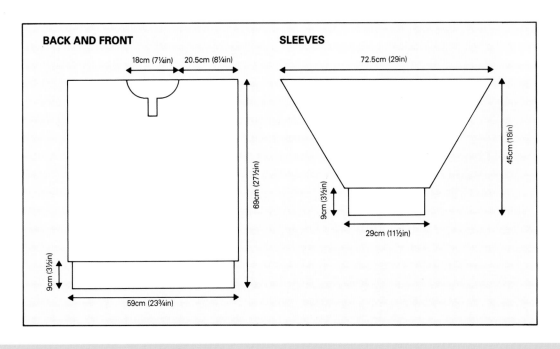

BACK AND FRONT

18cm (7¼in) · 20.5cm (8¼in)

69cm (27½in)

9cm (3½in)

59cm (23¾in)

SLEEVES

72.5cm (29in)

45cm (18in)

9cm (3½in)

29cm (11½in)

RIGHT SLEEVE

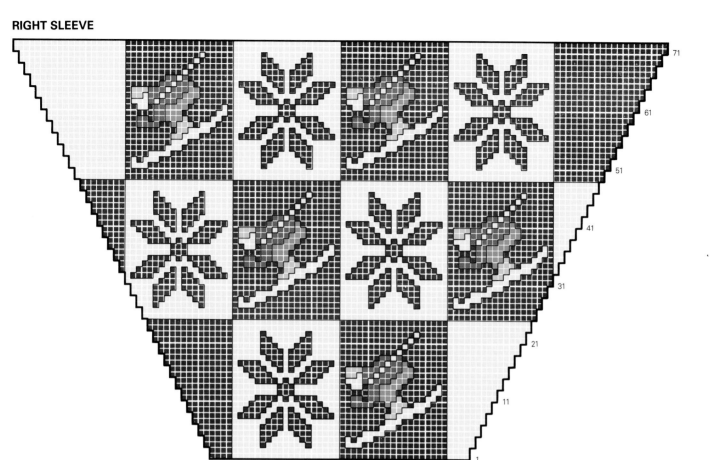

LEFT SLEEVE

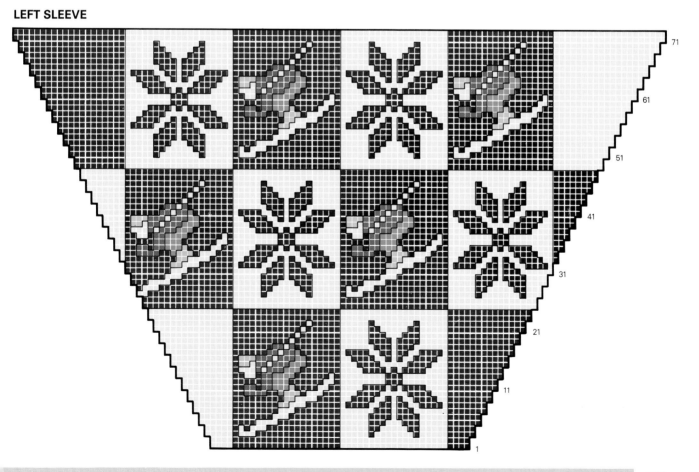

BACK

FRONT

CYCLING

TOURING

MATERIALS

Sunbeam *Pure New Wool DK*
50g (1¾oz) balls
3[4] balls No. 5951 (Beige) A
1 ball No. 5939 (Blue) B
1 ball No. 5935 (White) C
2 balls No. 5946 (Red/brown) D
1 ball No. 5942 (Mustard) E
1 ball No. 5970 (Emerald) F
1 ball No. 5914 (Dark Brown) G

Note *The yarns above are for the first size (woman's version). For yarns for the man's version, see HOW TO WORK FROM CHART.*

NEEDLES

1 pair of 4mm (US size 6) *or size to obtain correct tension/gauge*
4mm (US size 6) circular needle
1 pair of 3¼mm (US size 3)

TENSION/GAUGE

23 sts and 31 rows = 10cm (4in)
square measured over st st using
4mm (US size 6) needles
Check your tension/gauge before beginning.

MEASUREMENTS

To fit bust/chest size:
86-91[96-102]cm (34-36[38-40]in)
Actual width across back:
51[54]cm (20[22]in)
Length:
57[60]cm (23[24¼]in)
Figures for larger size are given in square brackets; where there is only one set of figures, it applies to both sizes.

HOW TO WORK FROM CHART

The yarns listed in the MATERIALS section and the colours used on the chart are for the first size (woman's version). For the 2nd size (man's version) substitute the colours as foll:

Use G for A, D for B, C for C, B for D, F for E, E for F and A for G, but working saddle of front biker in A and eye and mouth of back biker in B and D respectively.

BACK

The back is worked beg at lower left hand corner and increased and then decreased, ending at upper right hand corner.

With B and 4mm (US size 6) needles, cast on 2 sts and, changing to 4mm (US size 6) circular needle when there are too many sts to fit comfortably on needles, work back and forth in rows as foll:

Beg with a K row, work in st st foll chart for back from row 1 (reading this row and all odd-numbered rows as K rows from right to left and all even-numbered rows as P rows from left to right), using a separate ball or bobbin or yarn for each area of colour, twisting yarns when changing colours to prevent holes, and working incs as indicated, until chart row 109[115] has been completed, so ending with a RS row. 174[184] sts.

Cont foll chart working decs as indicated and omitting neck shaping which beg on row 140[146], until chart row 216[228] has been completed.

Cast (bind) off rem 2 sts.

FRONT

With B and 4mm (US size 6) needles, cast on 2 sts and, changing to 4mm (US size 6) circular needle when necessary, work back and forth in rows as foll:

Beg with a P row, work in st st foll chart from row 1 (reading this row and all odd-numbered rows as P rows from right to left and all even-numbered rows as K rows from left to right), working incs as indicated, until row 109 has been completed, so ending with a WS row.

Cont foll main chart working decs[incs] as indicated until row 114 has been completed. This sets position of bike rider.

Cont foll chart for shaping, but working bike rider from chart row 115 of uphill

bike rider for front until chart row 139[145] has been completed, so ending with a WS row. 126[136] sts.

Shape neck

Keeping patt correct, cast (bind) off 38[42] sts at beg of next row.

Cont shaping neck and working decs as indicated on main chart and foll uphill bike rider chart for motif, until chart row 216[228] has been completed.

Cast (bind) off rem 2 sts.

NECKBAND

Join left shoulder seam.

With D, 3¼mm (US size 3) needles and RS facing, pick up and K42[46] sts from back neck, 38[46] sts down left side of neck, 1 st at centre front and 38[46] sts up right side of neck. 119[139] sts.

Work in K1, P1 rib for 2.5cm (1in), dec I st at each side of centre front st on every alt row.

Cast (bind) off in rib.

ARMBANDS

Join right shoulder and neckband seams.

Place markers 23[25]cm (9[10]in) down from shoulders on back and front.

With D, 3¼mm (US size 3) needles and RS facing, pick up and K104[120] sts from between markers.

Work in K1, P1 rib for 2.5cm (1in).

Cast (bind) off in rib.

LOWER BANDS

With D, 3¼mm (US size 3) needles and RS facing, pick up and K100[110] along lower edge of front (opposite edge with neck shaping).

Work in K1, P1 rib for 6cm (2½in).

Cast (bind) off in rib.

Work lower band on back in the same way.

MAKING UP/ FINISHING

Sew side and armband seams. Press according to the instructions on the yarn label, omitting all ribbing, and keep one label for washing instructions.

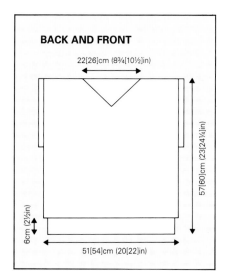

BACK AND FRONT

22[26]cm (8¾[10½]in)

57[60]cm (23[24¼]in)

6cm (2½in)

51[54]cm (20[22]in)

FRONT: UPHILL BIKE RIDER

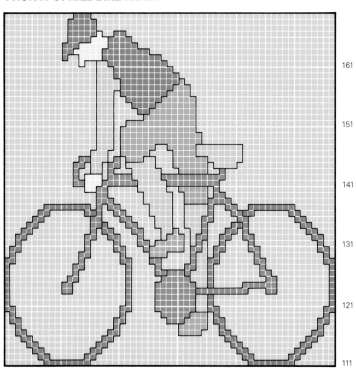

161

151

141

131

121

111

BACK AND FRONT

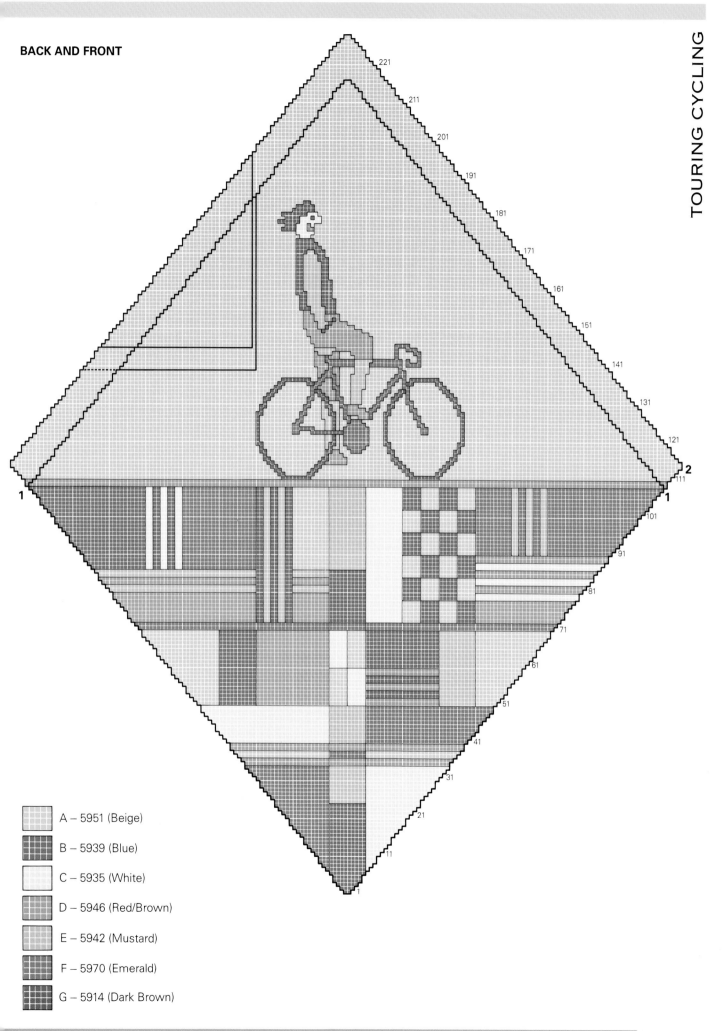

A – 5951 (Beige)

B – 5939 (Blue)

C – 5935 (White)

D – 5946 (Red/Brown)

E – 5942 (Mustard)

F – 5970 (Emerald)

G – 5914 (Dark Brown)

MOTOR RACING

MATERIALS

Sirdar *Sovereign Double Knitting*
50g (1¾oz) balls
11[12] balls No. 032 (Ivory) A
3 balls No. 013 (Black) B
1 ball No. 034 (Emerald) C
1 ball No. 042 (Flamenco) D
1 ball No. 066 (Mustard) E
1 ball No. 096 (Kingfisher) F

NEEDLES

1 pair 4mm (US size 6) *or size to
obtain correct tension/gauge*
1 pair 3¼mm (US size 3)

TENSION/GAUGE

23 sts and 28 rows = 10cm (4in)
square measured over st st using
4mm (US size 6) needles
*Check your tension/gauge before
beginning.*

MEASUREMENTS

To fit bust:
86-91[96-102]cm (34-36[38-40]in)
Actual width across back:
50[55]cm (20[22]in)
Length:
62[63]cm (25[25¼]in)
Sleeve length: 43cm (17in)
*Figures for larger size are given in
square brackets; where
there is only one set of figures, it
applies to both sizes.*

BACK

With A and 3¼mm (US size 3) needles, cast on 114[126] sts.
Beg check patt as foll:
Rows 1-4 *K3, P3, rep from * to end.
Rows 5-8 *P3, K3, rep from * to * end.
Rep rows 1-8 until 20 rows have been worked in all.
Change to 4mm (US size 6) needles and beg with a K row, work in st st foll chart for back from row 1, using a separate ball or bobbin of yarn for each area of colour and twisting yarns when changing colours to prevent holes, until chart row 154[156] has been completed, so ending with a WS row.
Shape Shoulders
Shape shoulders foll chart. Cast (bind) off rem 40 sts for back neck.

FRONT

Work as for back until chart row 100 has been completed, so ending with a WS row.
Shape Neck and Shoulders
Divide for neck on next row as foll:

Row 101 (RS) K37[43] sts, slip centre 40 sts onto a spare needle for front neck, using a separate ball of yarn K to end. Shape neck and shoulders foll chart.

SLEEVES

With A and 3¼mm (US size 3) needles, cast on 54[66] sts.
Work 20 rows in check patt as for back, inc 6[4] sts evenly across last row. 60[70]sts.
Change to 4mm (US size 6) needles and beg with a K row, work in st st foll sleeve chart from row 1 and working incs as indicated until chart row 100 has been completed. 90[100] sts.
Cast (bind) off.

RIGHT SIDE OF COLLAR

Join shoulder seams.
With RS facing, slip 40 sts of front neck from spare needle onto a 3¼mm (US size 3) needle.
With A, 3¼mm (US size 3) needles and RS facing, beg check patt as foll:

Row 1 (RS) K3, *P3, K3, rep from * to last st, K1.
Row 2 K1, *P3, K3, rep from * to last 3 sts, K3.
Rows 3 and 4 Rep last 2 rows once.
Row 5 K3, *K3, P3, rep from * to last st, K1.
Row 6 K4, *P3, K3, rep from * to end.
Rows 7 and 8 Rep last 2 rows once.
Rep rows 1-8 until collar is level with shoulder seam, ending at outer edge (edge with 3 st garter st band).
Beg dart shaping in garter st as foll:
Next 2 rows K to last 6 sts, turn, K to end.

□	A – 032 (Ivory)
▦	B – 013 (Black)
▦	C – 034 (Emerald)
▦	D – 042 (Flamenco)
▦	E – 066 (Mustard)
▦	F – 096 (Kingfisher)

SLEEVES

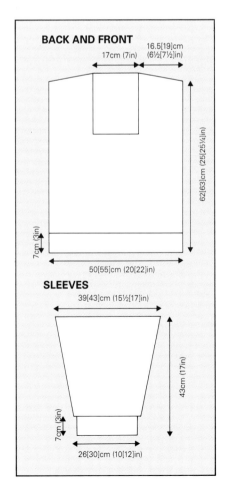

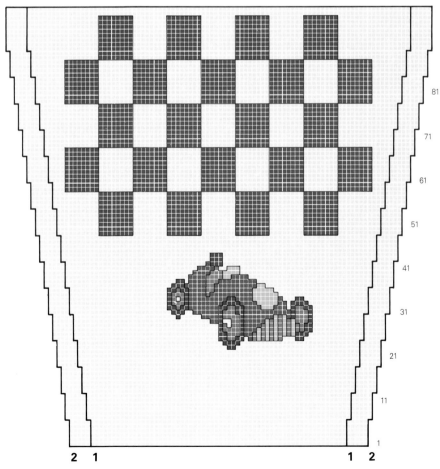

Next 2 rows K to last 12 sts, turn, K to end.

Cont in this way working 6 sts less each time until the pattern rows 'K to last 36 sts, turn, K to end of row' have been completed.

Next row Work in check patt across all 40 sts.

Work in check patt without shaping until collar fits to centre back neck.

Cast (bind) off in patt.

LEFT SIDE OF COLLAR

With A and 3¼mm (US size 3) needles, cast on 40 sts.

Beg check patt as foll:

Row 1 (RS) K1, *K3, P3, rep from * to last 3 sts, K3.

Complete as for right side of collar, but working check patt as set in row 1.

MAKING UP/ FINISHING

Sew both collar pieces onto neckline and join back seam. Join left side of collar to neckline under right side at front. Sew cast (bound) off edge of sleeves to back and front. Sew sleeve and side seams. Press according to the instructions on the yarn label, and keep one label for washing instructions.

BACK AND FRONT

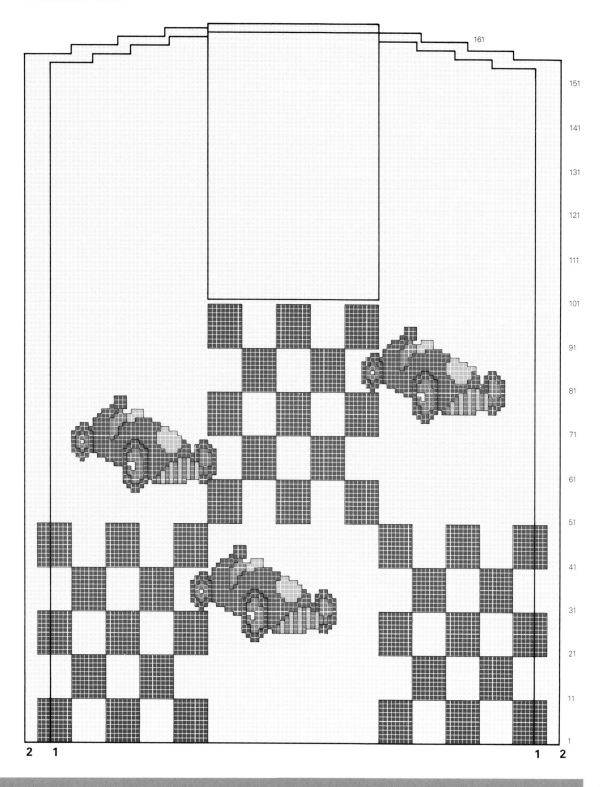

MATERIALS

Hayfield *Pure Wool Classics DK*
50g (1¾oz) balls
1 ball No. 002 (French Rose) A
4 balls No. 004 (Beaver) B
3[4] balls No. 008 (Maize) C
2 balls No. 020 (Tourmaline) D
6 balls No. 005 (Nutmeg) E
1 ball No. 021 (Opaline) F
1 ball No. 003 (Geranium) G
7 leather buttons

NEEDLES

1 pair 4mm (US size 6) *or size to obtain
correct tension/gauge*
1 pair 3¾mm (US size 5)

TENSION/GAUGE

22 sts and 28 rows = 10cm (4in)
square measured over st st using
4mm (US size 6) needles
*Check your tension/gauge before
beginning.*

HIKING

MEASUREMENTS

To fit bust:
86-9l[96-102]cm (34-36[38-40]in)
Actual width across back:
54[60]cm (21¾[23¾]in)
Length:
65cm (25¾in)
Sleeve seam:
40cm (16in)
*Figures for larger size
are given in
square brackets; where there
is only one set of
figures, it applies to both sizes.*

BACK

With C and 3¾mm (US size 5) needles, cast on 119[131] sts.

*Beg with a K row, work 10 rows in st st for hem, so ending with a P row.
P next row (RS) for hemline fold.
P 1 row.
Change to 4mm (US size 6) needles.*
Beg with a K row, work in st st foll chart for back from row 1, carrying background colour loosely across back of work when not in use and weaving it around working yarn, and using a separate ball or bobbin of yarn for each area of colour, twisting yarns when changing colours to prevent holes, until chart row 100 has been completed, so ending with a WS row.

Shape Armholes

Keeping patt correct throughout, shape armholes foll chart. 10 sts decreased at each side. 99[111] sts.
Cont foll chart until chart row 180 has been completed.
Cast (bind) off.

LEFT FRONT

With C and 3¾mm (US size 5) needles, cast on 54[60] sts.
Work as for back from * to *.
Beg with a K row, work in st st foll chart between markers for left front from row 1, until chart row 100 has been completed, so ending with a WS row.

Shape Armhole

Keeping patt correct throughout, shape armhole foll chart. 10 sts decreased at armhole edge. 44[50] sts.
Cont foll chart until chart row 130 has been completed, so ending with a WS row.

Shape Neck

Shape neck foll chart until chart row 180 has been completed.
Cast (bind) off rem 34[40] sts.

RIGHT FRONT

Work as for left front, but foll chart between markers for right front.

SLEEVES

With C and 3¾mm (US size 5) needles, cast on 67 sts (for both sizes).
Work as back from * to *.
Beg with a K row, work in st st foll sleeve chart from row 1 and working incs as indicated, until chart row 112 has

been completed, so ending with a WS row. 119 sts.

Shape Top of Sleeve

Keeping patt correct, shape top of sleeve foll chart until chart row 126 has been completed.
Cast (bind) off rem 91 sts.

BUTTON BAND

Join shoulder seams.
With C and 3¾mm (US size 5) needles, cast on 13 sts.
Work as for back from * to *.

Cont band as foll:
Row 1 K.
Row 2 (WS) K3, P1, work centre 5 sts foll chart row 2 between markers for front bands, P1, K3.

- A – 002 (French Rose)
- B – 004 (Beaver)
- C – 008 (Maize)
- D – 020 (Tourmaline)
- E – 005 (Nutmeg)
- F – 021 (Opaline)
- G – 003 (Geranium)

SLEEVES

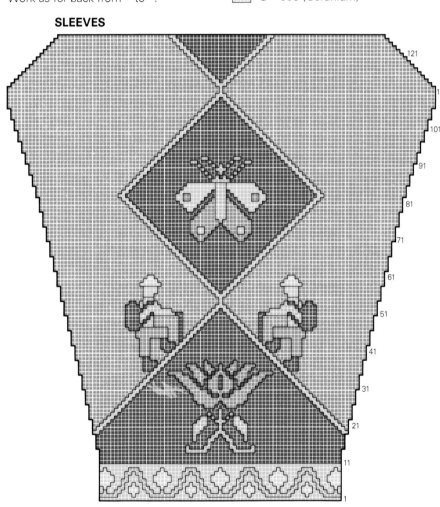

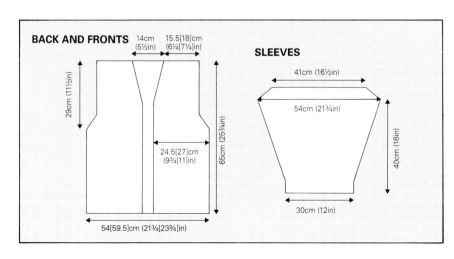

Row 3 K4, work centre 5 sts foll chart row 3, K4.

Cont in this way foll chart between markers for band until chart row 10 has been completed.

Row 11 (RS) With C, K.

Row 12 With C, K3, P7, K3.

Rows 13-20 Rep last 2 rows 4 times more.

These 20 rows form band patt.

Cont in patt until band, when slightly stretched, fits from lower edge of centre front to centre back neck.

Cast (bind) off in patt.

BUTTONHOLE BAND

Work as for button band, working the first one-stitch buttonhole on row 15 as foll:

Row 15 (buttonhole row 1) Work in patt to centre st, cast (bind) off centre st, work in patt to end.

Row 16 (buttonhole row 2) Work in patt, casting on 1 st over st cast (bound) off in last row.

Work 18 rows in patt.

Rep last 20 rows 5 times more, then work buttonhole rows 1 and 2 again.

Complete as for button band.

MAKING UP/ FINISHING

Sew sleeves into armholes. Sew sleeve seam and side seams. Turn up hems on back, fronts and sleeves to WS along hemline fold and sew down. Sew on front bands and join centre back seam. Sew on buttons.

Press according to the instructions on the yarn label, and keep one label for washing instructions.

BACK AND FRONTS

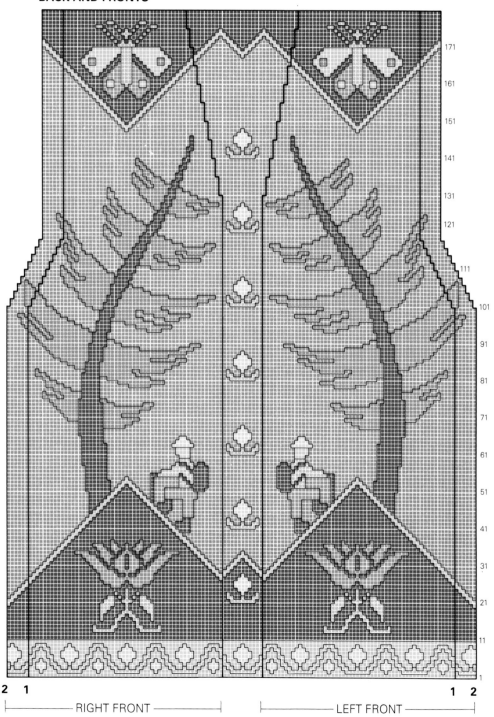

RIGHT FRONT   LEFT FRONT

FLYING
HEROES

MATERIALS

Rowan Yarns *Aran*
100g (3½oz) hanks
2[2:3] hanks No. 62 (Black) A
3[3:4] hanks No. 61 (Grey) B
2[2:3] hanks (Natural) C
1[1:2] hanks No. 111 (Blue) D
1 hank No. 113 (Yellow) E
1 hank No. 112 (Green) F
1 hank No. 114 (Red) G

NEEDLES

I pair 4½mm (US size 7) *or size to
obtain correct tension/gauge*
I pair 3¾mm (US size 5)

TENSION/GAUGE

I9 sts and 24 rows = 10cm (4in) square
measured over st st
using 4½mm (US size 7) needles
*Check your tension/gauge before
beginning.*

MEASUREMENTS

To fit bust:
9I[102:112]cm (36[40:44]in)
Actual width across back:
53[58:63]cm (21[23:25]in)
Length:
63cm (25in)
Sleeve length:
44cm (17½in)
*Figures for larger sizes are given
in square brackets; where
there is only one set of figures, it
applies to all sizes.*

BACK

With C and 3¾mm (US size 5) needles, cast on 18[23:28] sts, then change to A and cast on 82[87:92] sts more. 100[110:120] sts.

Using A for the A sts and C for the C sts throughout and twisting yarns when changing colours to prevent holes, beg K2, P2 rib as foll:

Rib row 1 P1, *K2, P2, rep from *, ending with K2[1:2], P1[0:1].

Rib row 2 K the K sts and P the P sts.

Keeping colours correct, rep last row until 12 rows have been worked in all.

Change to 4½mm (US size 7) needles and beg with a K row, work in st st foll chart for back from row 1, using a separate ball or bobbin of yarn for each area of colour and twisting yarns when changing colours to prevent holes, until chart row 140 has been completed.

Cast (bind) off in the correct colours.

FRONT

Work as for back until chart row 128 has been completed, ending with a WS row.

Shape Neck

Keeping patt correct, shape neck foll chart slipping 20 centre sts onto a spare needle, until chart row 140 has been completed.

Cast (bind) off rem 30[35:40] sts (at each side of neck).

SLEEVES

With B and 3¾mm (US size 5) needles, cast on 26[30:34] sts, then change to C and cast on 26[30:34] sts more. 52[60:68] sts.

Using C for the C sts and B for the B sts throughout, beg K2, P2 rib as foll:

Rib row 1 P1, *K2, P2, rep from *, ending with K2, P1.

Rib row 2 K the K sts and P the P sts.

Keeping colours correct, rep last row until 12 rows have been worked in all.

Change to 4½mm (US size 7) needles and beg with a K row, work in st st foll sleeve chart from row 1 and working incs as indicated, until chart row 94 has been completed. 82[90:98] sts.

Cast (bind) off.

NECKBAND

Join right shoulder seam.

With B, 3¾mm (US size 5) needles and RS facing, pick up and K20 sts down left side of front neck, 20 sts from centre, 20 sts up right side of front neck and 38 sts from back neck. 98 sts.

Beg K2, P2 rib as foll:

Rib row 1 (WS) P2, *K2, P2, rep from * to end.

Rib row 2 K the K sts and P the P sts.

Rep last row until 7 rows have been worked in all.

Cast (bind) off loosely in rib.

MAKING UP/ FINISHING

Join the left shoulder seam and neckband.

Sew cast (bound) off edge of sleeves to back and front. Sew sleeve and side seams.

Press according to the instructions on the yarn label, omitting all ribbing on garment, and keep one yarn label for washing instructions.

SLEEVES

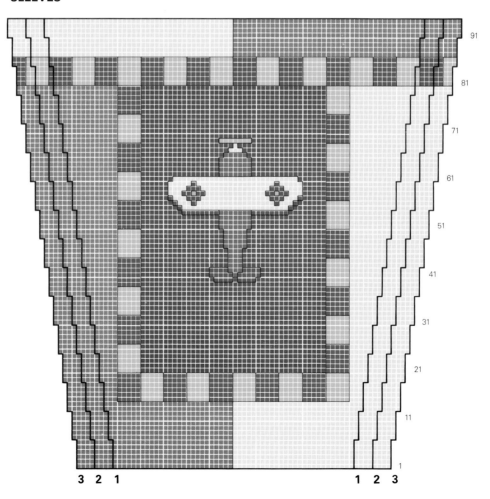

3 2 1   1 2 3

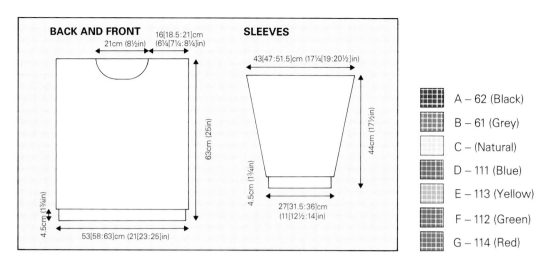

BACK AND FRONT

SLEEVES

16[18.5:21]cm (6¼[7¼:8¼]in)
21cm (8½in)
43[47:51.5]cm (17¼[19:20½]in)
63cm (25in)
44cm (17½in)
4.5cm (1¾in)
4.5cm (1¾in)
27[31.5:36]cm (11[12½:14]in)
53[58:63]cm (21[23:25]in)

A – 62 (Black)
B – 61 (Grey)
C – (Natural)
D – 111 (Blue)
E – 113 (Yellow)
F – 112 (Green)
G – 114 (Red)

BACK AND FRONT

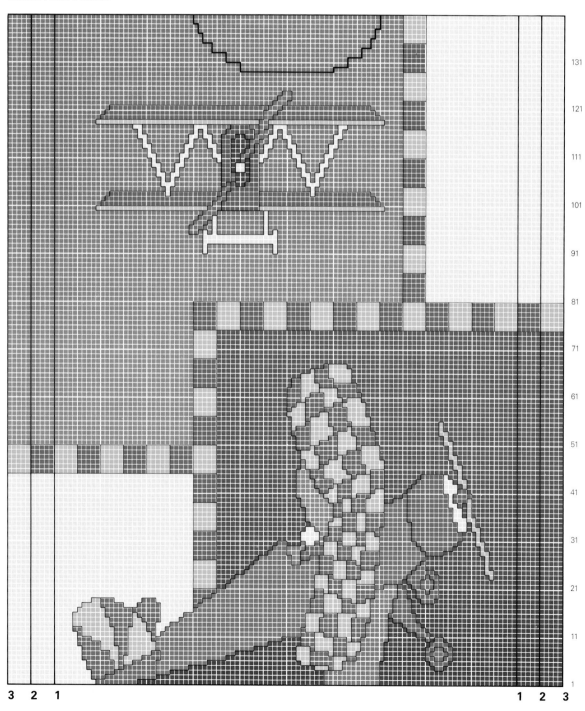

MATERIALS

Emu *Superwash DK*
50g (1¾oz) balls
8[9:9] balls No. 3079 (Cream) A
5[5:6] balls No. 3099 (Brown) B
1 ball No. 3071 (Grey-blue) C
1 toggle

NEEDLES

1 pair 4mm (US size 6) *or size to obtain
correct tension/gauge*
1 pair 3¾mm (US size 5)
1 pair 3¼mm (US size 3)

TENSION/GAUGE

23 sts and 28 rows = 10cm (4in)
square measured over st st using
4mm (US size 6) needles
*Check your tension/gauge
before beginning.*

MEASUREMENTS

To fit bust:
87[91:96]cm (34[36:38]in)
Actual width across back at underarm:
48[50:53]cm (19¼[20¼:21¼]in)
Length:
59[60:61]cm (23½[23¾:24]in)
Sleeve length (with cuff turned back):
45cm (18in)
*Figures for larger sizes are given
in square brackets; where
there is only one set of figures, it
applies to all sizes.*

RIDING GREATS

BACK

With C and 3¼mm (US size 3) needles, cast on 100[106:112] sts.
K 8 rows (garter st).

Change to 3¾mm (US size 5) needles and beg with a K row, work in st st foll chart for back from row 1, carrying background colour loosely across back of work when not in use and weaving it around working yarn, using a separate length yarn for each motif, twisting yarns when changing colours to prevent holes, and working incs as indicated until chart row 24 has been completed, so ending with a WS row. 104[110:116] sts.

Change to 4mm (US size 6) needles and cont foll chart, working incs as indicated until chart row 164[166:168] has been completed, so ending with a WS row. 110[116:122] sts.

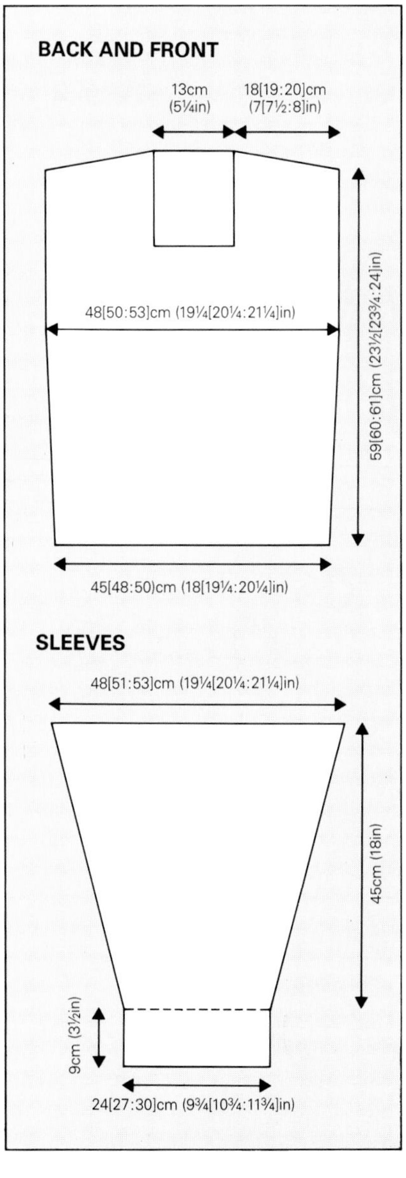

Shape Shoulders

Keeping patt correct, shape shoulders foll chart. Cast (bind) off rem 30 sts for back neck.

FRONT

Work as for back until chart row 102 has been completed, so ending with a WS row. 110[116:122] sts.

Shape Neck and Shoulders

Divide for neck on next row as foll:
Row 103 (RS) Work 40[43:46] sts in patt, cast (bind) off centre 30 sts, work in patt to end.
Keeping patt correct, shape neck and shoulders foll chart.

SLEEVES

SLEEVES

With C and 3¼mm (US size 3) needles, cast on 56[62:68] sts.
K 8 rows (garter st).

Change to 3¾mm (US size 5) needles and work in st st, foll cuff chart from row 1 until chart row 23 has been completed. With B, K 1 row (WS) for hemline fold. Break off B.

Slip all sts back on to empty needle.
With A and with WS still facing, P 1 row.
Change to 4mm (US size 6) needles and beg with a K row, work in st st foll sleeve chart from row 1 and working incs as indicated until chart row 124 has been completed. 110[116:122] sts.

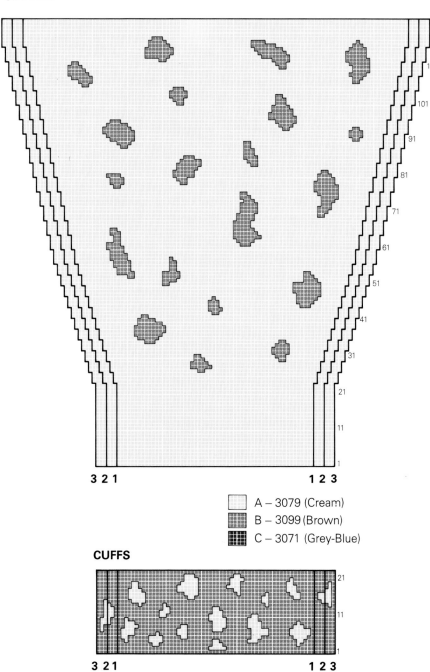

BACK AND FRONT

13cm (5¼in) 18[19:20]cm (7[7½:8]in)

48[50:53]cm (19¼[20¼:21¼]in)

59[60:61]cm (23½[23¾:24]in)

45[48:50]cm (18[19¼:20¼]in)

SLEEVES

48[51:53]cm (19¼[20¼:21¼]in)

45cm (18in)

9cm (3½in)

24[27:30]cm (9¾[10¾:11¾]in)

121
111
101
91
81
71
61
51
41
31
21
11
1

3 2 1   1 2 3

A – 3079 (Cream)
B – 3099 (Brown)
C – 3071 (Grey-Blue)

CUFFS

21

11

1

3 2 1   1 2 3

Cast (bind) off.

RIGHT SIDE OF COLLAR

Join right shoulder seam.
With B, 3¼mm (US size 3) needles and RS facing, pick up and K63[65:67] sts up right side of neck (marking last st for shoulder seam point) and 20 sts to centre back neck, leaving cast (bound) off edge of centre front neck unworked. 83[85:87] sts.
K every row (garter st), inc I st at marked shoulder seam point on every 6th row 9 times in all. 92[94:96] sts.
Cont to K every row until collar is deep

enough to fit across all the cast (bound) off sts at centre front.
Cast (bind) off.

LEFT SIDE OF COLLAR

Join left shoulder seam.
With B, 3¼mm (US size 3) needles and RS facing, pick up and K20 sts from centre back neck to shoulder seam and (marking next st for shoulder seam point) 63[65:67] sts down left side of neck, leaving cast (bound) off edge of centre front neck unworked. 83[85:87] sts.
Complete as for right side of collar.

MAKING UP/ FINISHING

Sew cast (bound) off edge of sleeves to back and front. Sew sleeve and side seams, turning back cuffs. Sew edge of right side of collar to cast (bound) off edge of centre front neck. Sew edge of left side of collar to centre front neck under right side. Join back seam of collar. Attach toggle as shown, sewing through both thicknesses of collar to secure 7cm (2¾in) above centre front neck.
Press according to the instructions on the yarn label, and keep one label for washing instructions.

BACK AND FRONT

161
151
141
131
121
111
101
91
81
71
61
51
41
31
21
11
1

3 2 1   1 2 3

TOE

MATERIALS

Jaeger *Angora Spun*
20g (¾oz) balls
13[14] balls No. 585 (Scarlet) A
3[4] balls No. 588 (Cream) B
1 ball No. 594 (Cobalt) C
1 ball No. 593 (Topaz) D
1 ball No. 589 (Jade) E
1 ball No. 591 (Navy) F
One press stud (snap) for collar

NEEDLES

1 pair 3¾mm (US size 5) *or size to*
obtain correct tension/gauge
1 pair 3¾mm (US size 3)

TENSION/GAUGE

27 sts and 35 rows = 10cm (4in)
square measured over background
colour patt using 3¾mm
(US size 5) needles
Check your tension/gauge before beginning.

MEASUREMENTS

To fit bust:
86-91[96-102]cm (34-36[38-40]in)
Actual width across back:
51[56]cm (20[22]in)
Length:
61[63]cm (24[25]in)
Sleeve length:
45[48]cm (18[19]in)
Figures for larger size are given
in square brackets; where
there is only one set of figures,
it applies to both sizes.

FRONT

With A and 3mm (US size 3) needles, cast on 117[131] sts.
Beg moss (seed) st as foll:
Row 1 K1, *P1, K1, rep from * to end.
Rep last row 15 times more, inc 20 sts evenly across last row. 137[151] sts.
Change to 3¾mm (US size 5) needles.**
Beg with a K row, work in st st foll chart for front from row 1, carrying B loosely across back of work when not in use and weaving it around working yarn, and using a separate ball or bobbin of yarn for each area of colour, twisting yarns when changing colours to prevent holes, until chart row 120 has been completed, so ending with a WS row.

Shape Armholes

Keeping patt correct throughout, shape armholes foll chart. 15 sts decreased at each side. 107[121] sts.
Work without shaping, until chart row 154[160] has been completed, so ending with a WS row.

Shape Neck

Shape neck foll chart until chart row 200[206] has been completed.
Cast (bind) off rem 35[42] sts (at each side of neck).

BACK

Work as for front to **.
Beg with a K row, work in st st foll chart from row 1, but only working one pattern block (43 sts) on lower left of chart and keeping background in A and B as set, until chart row 120 has been completed. Shape armhole as for front, then work without shaping in patt, omitting front neck shaping, until chart row 200[206] is complete. Cast (bind) off.

SLEEVES

With A and 3mm (US size 3) needles, cast on 55[61] sts. Work 16 rows in moss (seed) st as for front, inc 20 sts evenly across last row. 75[81] sts.

Change to 3¾mm (US size 5) needles and beg with a K row, work in st st foll sleeve chart from row 11[1] and working incs as indicated, until chart row 154 has been completed, so ending with a WS row. 117[127] sts.

Shape Top of Sleeve

Keeping patt correct, shape top of sleeve foll chart until chart row 171 has been completed. 83[93] sts.
With A, purl 1 row and cast (bind) off.

COLLAR (2 PIECES)

With A and 3mm (US size 3) needles, cast on 8 sts.
Beg moss (seed) st as foll:
Row 1 *K1, P1, rep from * to end.
Row 2 P the K sts, and K the P sts.

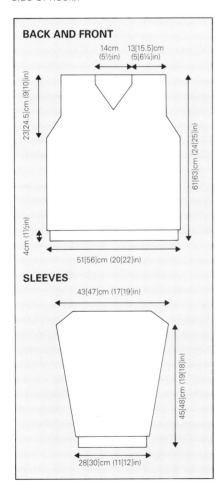

BACK AND FRONT

14cm (5½in) 13[15.5]cm (5[6¼]in)

23[24.5]cm (9[10]in)

61[63]cm (24[25]in)

4cm (1½in)

51[56]cm (20[22]in)

SLEEVES

43[47]cm (17[19]in)

45[48]cm (19[18]in)

28[30]cm (11[12]in)

SLEEVES

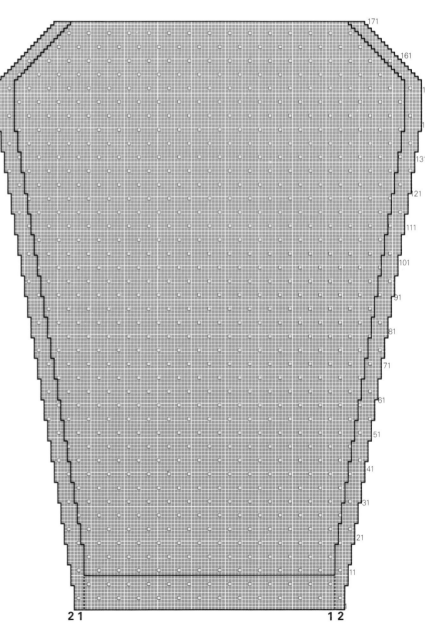

171

161

151

141

131

121

111

101

91

81

71

61

51

41

31

21

11

2 1   1 2

Rep last row to form moss (seed) st patt.

Work 1 row in moss (seed) st.

Keeping moss (seed) st patt correct throughout and keeping one side straight, inc l st at beg of next row and every foll 4th row until there are 26 sts. Work without shaping until shaped edge of collar fits from centre front to shoulder seam, ending at straight edge.

Shape Back Neck

Cast on 22 sts at end of next row (shaped edge). 48 sts.

Work without shaping for 7.5cm (3in). Cast (bind) off loosely in moss (seed) st. Make another piece in the same way, reversing front neck shaping.

MAKING UP/ FINISHING

Join shoulder seams. Sew sleeves into armholes, matching decs. Sew sleeve and side seams. Sew shaped edge of one half of collar onto right side of front neckline, joining 8 cast-on sts to centre sts at beg of neck shaping. Sew 22 cast-on sts onto half of back neck. Sewing 8 cast-on sts behind those of first piece, rep with second piece of collar and join back seam. Sew a press stud (snap) onto the collar, and decorate with 2 small pompons in B as shown. Press according to the instructions on the yarn label, omitting moss (seed) st, and keep one label for washing instructions.

BACK AND FRONT

A – 585 (Scarlet)
B – 588 (Cream)
C – 594 (Cobalt)
D – 593 (Topaz)
E – 589 (Jade)
F – 591 (Navy)

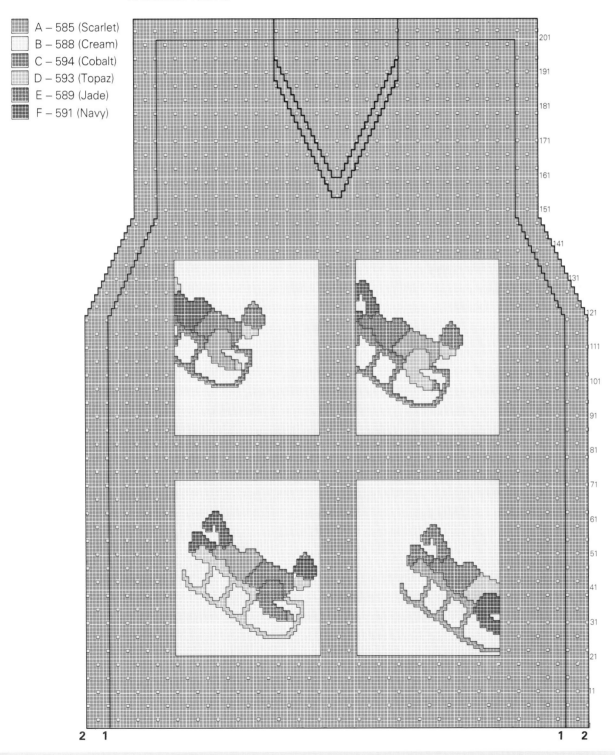

CRICKETING GREATS

MATERIALS

Argyll *Viscount DK*
50g (1¾oz) balls
9[9:10] balls No. 740 (Cream)

NEEDLES

1 pair 4mm (US size 6) *or size to obtain
correct tension/gauge*
1 pair 3¼mm (US size 3)
Cable needle

TENSION/GAUGE

22 sts and 28 rows = 10cm (4in)
square measured over st st using
4mm (US size 6) needles
30 sts and 32 rows = 10cm (4in)
square measured over patt slightly
stretched using 4mm (US size 6)
needles
*Check your tension/gauge
before beginning.*

MEASUREMENTS

To fit chest/bust:
86-91[96-102:107-112]cm
(34-36[38-40:
42-44]in)
Actual width across back:
45[49:53]cm (18[19¾:21¼]in)
Length:
64cm (25½in)
*Figures for larger sizes are given
in square brackets; where
there is only one set of figures, it
applies to all sizes.*

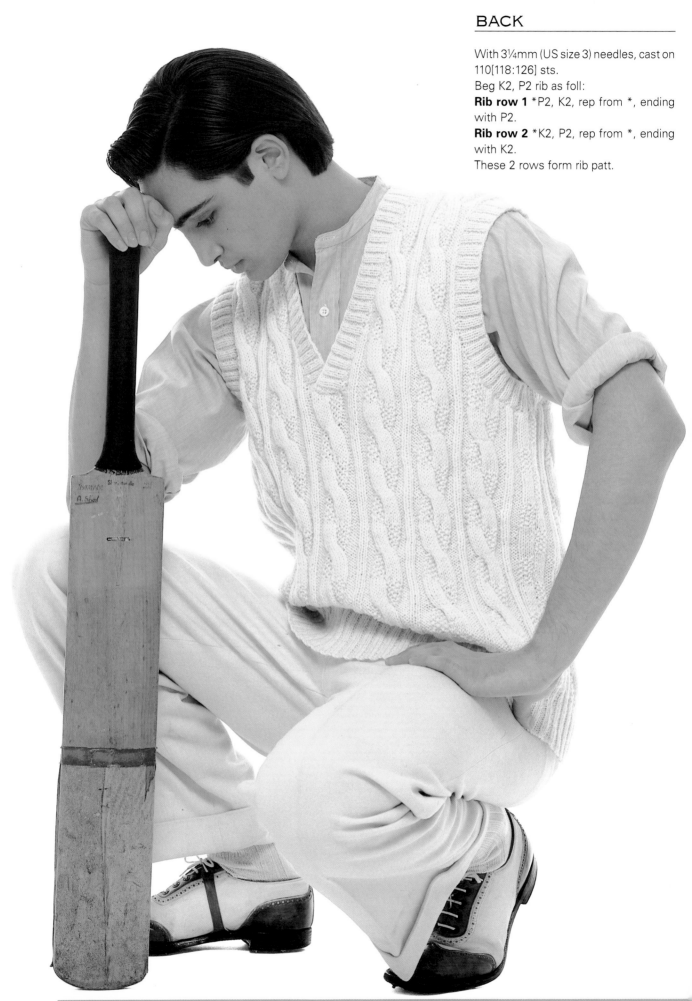

BACK

With 3¼mm (US size 3) needles, cast on 110[118:126] sts.
Beg K2, P2 rib as foll:
Rib row 1 *P2, K2, rep from *, ending with P2.
Rib row 2 *K2, P2, rep from *, ending with K2.
These 2 rows form rib patt.

Cont in rib patt until 23 rows have been completed from cast on.

1st size only:

Rib row 24 K into front and back of first st, K1, *(P2, K2) twice, (P2, K into front and back of each of next 2 sts) twice*, rep from * to * 5 times, ending (P2, K2) twice, P2, K1, K into front and back of last st. 136 sts.

2nd size only:

Rib row 24 K into front and back of each of first 2 sts, P2, K into front and back of next st, K1, rep from * to * on rib row 24 of first size 6 times, ending (P2, K2) twice, P2, K into front and back of next st, K1, P2, K into front and back of each of last 2 sts. 148 sts.

3rd size:

Rib row 24 K2, P into front and back of next st, P1, K into front and back of each of next 2 sts, P2, K into front and back of each of next 2 sts, rep from * to * on rib row 24 of first size 7 times, ending P1, P into front and back of next st, K2. 160 sts.

All sizes:

Change to 4mm (US size 6) needles and work in patt foll chart from row 1, beg at marker on right of chart indicated for your chosen size, working to the end of the 20 patt sts and rep 20 patt sts to last 13[19:25] sts, then working from end of patt rep to marker on left indicated for your chosen size. 136[148:160] sts.

Cont in this way foll chart between markers for chosen size until chart row 10 has been completed.

Work cables along next row as foll:

Patt row 11 (cable row) Work first 3[9:15] sts in patt foll chart, *slip next 5 sts on to a cn and hold in front, (P1, K1) twice, P1, then K5 sts from cn, work next 10 sts in patt foll chart*, rep from * to * to last 13[19:25] sts, work to end foll chart.

Cont foll chart from row 12 until all 20 chart rows have been completed.

Rep chart rows 1-20 until 100 rows have been completed in patt (5 patt repeats), so ending with a WS row.**

Shape Armholes

Keeping patt correct throughout, cast (bind) off 4[5:6] sts at beg of next 2 rows, 3[4:5] sts at beg of next 2 rows, 2[3:4] sts at beg of next 2 rows, 2[3:3] sts at beg of next 2 rows, 2[2:3] sts at beg of next 2 rows, 1[2:2] sts at beg of next 2 rows, 1[1:2] sts at beg of next 2 rows.

Dec 1 st at beg of next 4[6:8] rows.

17[23:29] sts decreased in all at each

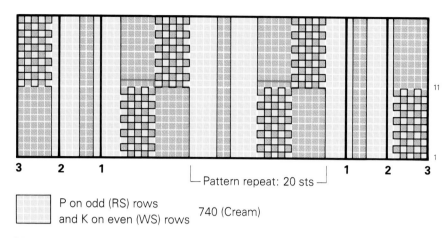

3 2 1

⌐ Pattern repeat: 20 sts ⌐

1 2 3

☐ P on odd (RS) rows and K on even (WS) rows

740 (Cream)

⌐ cable crossing st

▦ K on odd (RS) rows and P on even (WS) rows

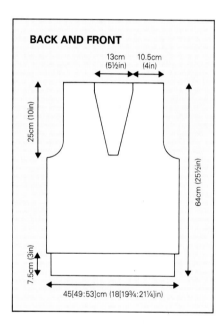

BACK AND FRONT

13cm (5½in)   10.5cm (4in)

25cm (10in)

64cm (25½in)

7.5cm (3in)

45[49:53]cm (18[19¾:21¼]in)

side. 102 sts.

Cont in patt until 9 patt repeats have been completed in all.

Cast (bind) off in patt.

FRONT

Work as for back to **.

Shape Neck and Shoulder

Next row (RS) Cast (bind) off 4[5:6] sts, work 59[64:69] sts in patt including st already on needle after cast (bind) off, turn, leaving rem 73[79:85] sts on a spare needle.

Keeping patt correct throughout, cont working armhole shaping to match back, AND AT THE SAME TIME work neck shaping on first side of neck as foll:

Dec 1 st at beg of next row (neck edge) and cont to dec 1 st at neck edge on 5th and every foll 5th row 13 times more. 15 sts decreased in all at neck edge. 31 sts.

Complete to match back.

Return to sts on spare needle and with RS facing, rejoin yarn and cast (bind) off 10 sts, cont in patt to end of row.

Work armhole, neck and shoulder shaping to match first side.

ARMBANDS

Join shoulder seams.

With 3¼mm (US size 3) needles and RS facing, pick up and K88 sts from front armhole edge and 88 sts from back armhole edge. 176 sts.

Work 10 rows in K2, P2 rib.

Cast (bind) off in rib.

NECKBAND

With 3¼mm (US size 3) needles and RS facing, pick up and K100 sts along right neck edge (omitting 10 centre sts) to centre back neck.

Beg K2, P2 rib as foll:

Rib row 1 K1,* P2, K2, rep from *, ending P2, K1.

Rib row 2 K the K sts and P the P sts.

These 2 rows form rib patt.

Work 8 rows more in rib.

Cast (bind) off in rib.

Rep to match on left side of neck.

MAKING UP/ FINISHING

Overlap neckband and sew on to the 10 cast (bound) off sts at centre front. Sew back seam on neckband. Sew side and armband seams. Block to size and press according to the instructions on the yarn label, omitting all ribbing, and keep one label for washing instructions.

MATERIALS

Emu *Superwash DK*
50g (1¾oz) balls
6[6:7] balls No. 3053 (Navy) A
2[3:3] balls No. 3054 (Blue) B
3[3:4] balls No. 3072 (Peacock) C
3[3:4] balls No. 3073 (Light Green) D
1 ball No. 3007 (Peach) E
I ball No. 3032 (Rose) F
I ball No. 3048 (Mauve) G
1 ball No. 3012 (Gold) H
1 ball No. 3014 (Russett) J
6 buttons

NEEDLES

1 pair 4mm (US size 6) *or size to obtain
correct tension/gauge*
1 pair 3¼mm (US size 3)

TENSION/GAUGE

22 sts and 28 rows = 10cm (4in)
square measured over st st using
4mm (US size 6) needles
*Check your tension/gauge before
beginning.*

MEASUREMENTS

To fit bust:
91[102:112]cm (36[40:44]in)
Actual width across back:
50[55:59]cm (20[22:23½]in)
Length:
68cm (27¼in)
Sleeve length:
50[52:53]cm (20¾[20:21¼]in)
*Figures for larger sizes are
given in square
brackets; where there
is only one set
of figures, it applies
to all sizes.*

FISHING GREATS

BACK

With A and 3¼mm (US size 3) needles, cast on 100[110:120] sts.

Work in K1, P1 rib for 7.5cm (3in), inc 10 sts evenly across last row. 110[120:130] sts.

Change to 4mm (US size 6) needles and beg with a K row, work in st st foll chart for back from row 1, using a separate ball or bobbin of yarn for each area of colour and twisting yarns when changing colours to prevent holes, until chart row 170 has been completed.

Cast (bind) off.

A – 3053 (Navy)

B – 3054 (Blue)

C – 3072 (Peacock)

D – 3073 (Light Green)

E – 3007 (Peach)

F – 3032 (Rose)

G – 3048 (Mauve)

H – 3012 (Gold)

J – 3014 (Russett)

BACK

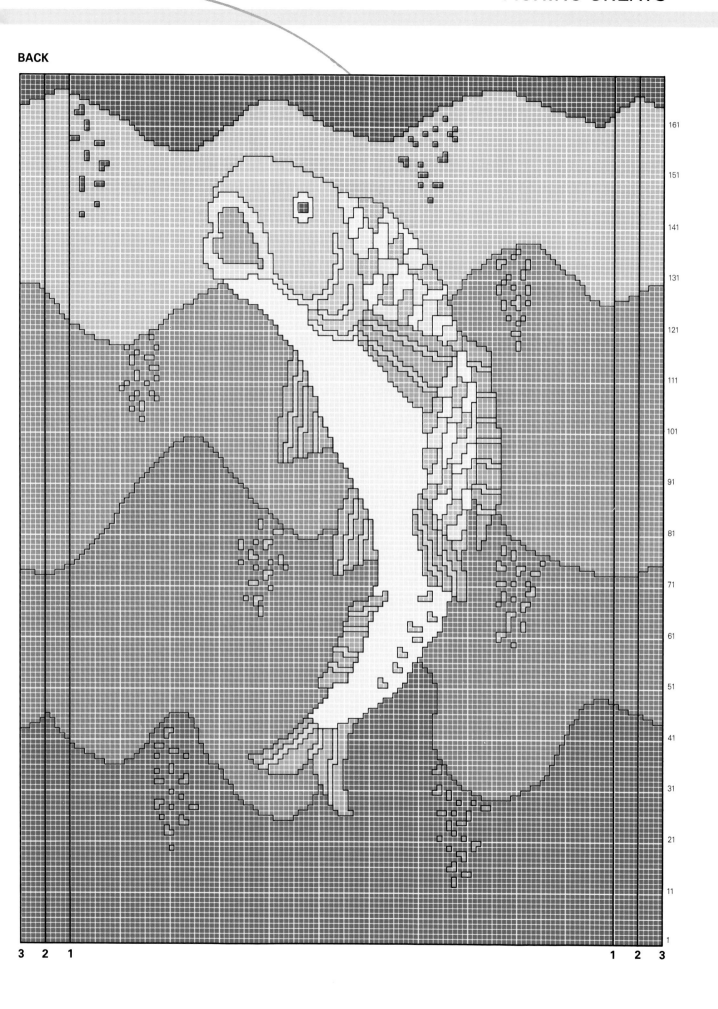

3 2 1   1 2 3

LEFT FRONT

With A and 3¼mm (US size 3) needles, cast on 46[50:56] sts.

Work in K1, P1 rib for 7.5cm (3in), inc 4[5:4] sts evenly across last row. 50[55:60] sts.

Change to 4mm (US size 6) needles and beg with a K row, work in st st foll chart for left front from row 1 until chart row 45 has been completed, so ending with a RS row.

Pocket

Row 46 (WS) With B, P14 and slip these sts on to a st holder; K22 sts for pocket to form foldline; P to end and slip these 14[19:24] sts on to a 2nd st holder. Do not break off yarn.

With a separate ball of B, cont on these 22 sts and beg with a K row, work 90 rows in st st, ending with a P row. Break off yarn.

Row 47 (RS) With B, K14[19:24] sts from st holder, K22 sts of pocket, K14 sts from rem st holder.

Cont foll chart from row 48, until chart row 81 has been completed, so ending with a RS row.

Shape Neck

Keeping patt correct, shape neck foll chart, until chart row 170 has been completed.

Cast (bind) off rem 40[45:50] sts.

RIGHT FRONT

Work as for left front, but foll chart for right front, reversing position of pocket and working 1 row less before beg neck shaping.

SLEEVES

With A and 3¼mm (US size 3) needles, cast on 44[50:56] sts.

Work in K1, P1 rib for 7.5cm (3in), inc 16 sts evenly across last row. 60[66:72]sts.

Change to 4mm (US size 6) needles and beg with a K row, work in st st foll sleeve chart from row 41[37:33] working incs as indicated until chart row 160 is complete. 98[104:110] sts. Cast (bind) off.

LEFT FRONT BAND AND COLLAR

Join shoulder seams.

With A and 3¼mm (US size 3) needles, cast on 15 sts.

Work in K1, P1 rib until band fits from lower edge of centre front to beg of neck shaping.

Keeping rib patt correct throughout, inc 1 st on inner edge on next row and every foll alt row until there are 34 sts, then cont inc 1 st on every 4th row until there are 46 sts.

Work without shaping until band and collar fit to shoulder seam, ending at outer edge.

Beg dart shaping as foll:

Next 2 rows Rib to last 6 sts, turn, rib to end.

Next 2 rows Rib to last 12 sts, turn, rib to end.

Cont in this way, ribbing 6 sts less each time, until the rows 'rib to last 42 sts, turn, rib to end' have been worked.

Next row Rib across all 46 sts.

Work without shaping until collar fits to centre back neck.

Cast (bind) off in rib.

RIGHT FRONT BAND AND COLLAR

Mark the position of 6 buttons on left front band, the first 6 rows from cast on edge, the last at beg of neck shaping with rem 4 evenly spaced between.

Work right front band as for left front band, working buttonholes to correspond with markers as foll:

Row 7 (RS) Rib 6 sts, cast (bind) off 2 sts, rib to end.

Row 8 Rib to end, casting on 2 sts over those cast (bound) off in last row.

Complete as for the left front band and collar.

MAKING UP/ FINISHING

Sew on front bands and collar and join back seam on collar. Sew cast (bound) off edge of sleeves to back and front. Sew sleeve and side seams. Sew pocket bag sides and attach lightly at each corner to the front. Sew on buttons.

Press according to the instructions on the yarn label, omitting all ribbing, and keep one label for washing instructions.

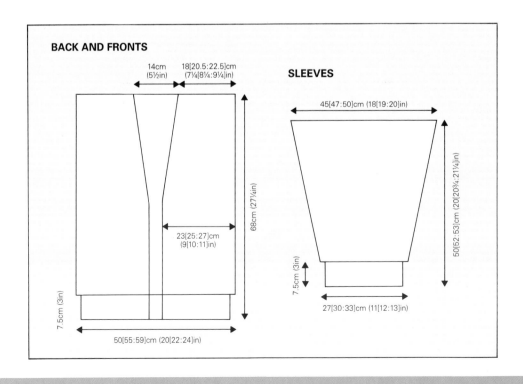

FRONT AND SLEEVES

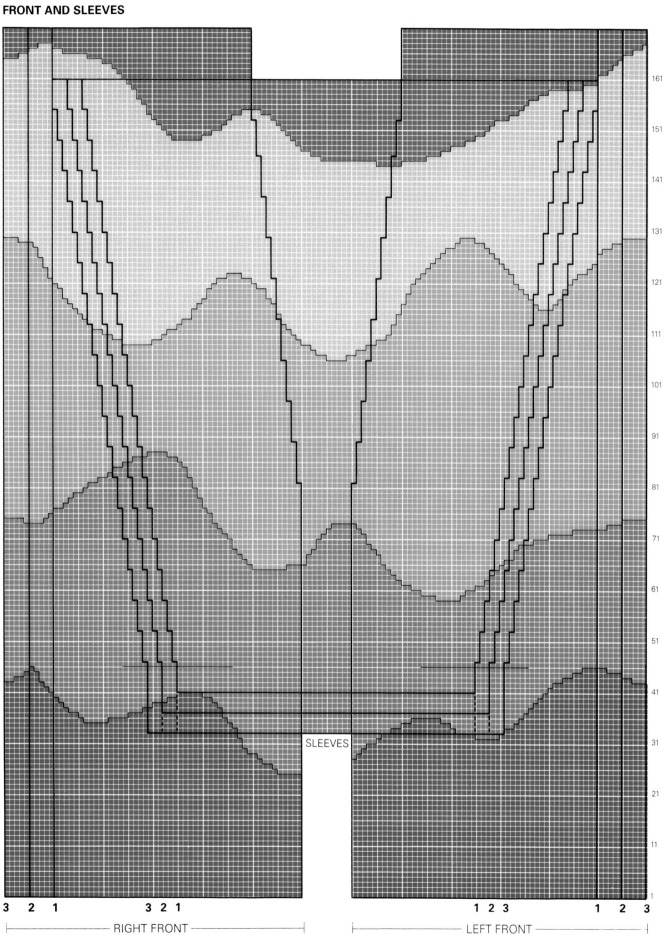

SLEEVES

3   2   1   3 2 1   1 2 3   1   2   3

|——— RIGHT FRONT ———| |——————— LEFT FRONT ———————|

MATERIALS

Rowan *Aran*
100g (3½oz) hanks
7[7:8] hanks No. 504 (Admiral) A
1 hank No. 503 (Comanche) B
1 hank No. 002 (Natural) C
1 hank No. 111 (Royal) D
1 hank No. 610 (Peppercorn) E
50cm (20in) navy blue open-ended
zipper
2 buttons

NEEDLES

4½mm (US size 7) *or size to obtain
correct tension gauge*
4½mm (US size 7) circular needle
1 pair 3¾mm (US size 5)

TENSION/GAUGE

19 sts and 24 rows = 10cm (4in)
square measured over st st using
4½mm (US size 7) needles
*Check your tension/gauge before
beginning.*

MEASUREMENTS

To fit bust:
86-91[96-102:107-112]
(34-36[38-40:
42-44]in)
Actual width across back at underarm:
60[65:71]cm (24[26:28¼]in)
Length:
62cm (24½in)
Width from cuff edge to cuff edge:
140cm (56in)
*Figures for larger sizes are given
in square brackets; where
there is only one set of figures, it
applies to all sizes.*

CANOEING

BACK

With A and 3¾mm (US size 5) needles, cast on 94[104:114] sts.

Work 16 rows in K1, P1 rib, inc 10 sts evenly across last row. 104[114:124] sts.

Change to 4½mm (US size 7) needles and beg with a K row, work in st st foll chart for back from row 1, using a separate ball or bobbin of yarn for each area of colour, twisting yarns when changing colours to prevent holes, and working incs as indicated until chart row 66 has been completed, so ending with a WS row. 114[124:134] sts.

Shape Sleeves

Change to 4½mm (US size 7) circular needle and working back and forth in rows and keeping patt correct throughout, shape sleeves foll chart until chart row 132 has been completed. 242 sts.

Slip sts on to a spare needle.

POCKET LININGS

With A and 4½mm (US size 7) needles, cast on 20 sts.

Beg with a K row, work 27 rows in st st, so ending with a K row.

Slip sts on to a spare needle.

Make a 2nd lining in the same way.

POCKET FLAPS

With A and 4½mm (US size 7) needles, cast on 10 sts.

Row 1 (RS) K into front and back of first st, K to last st, K into front and back of last st.

Row 2 As first row.

Row 3 K3, K into front and back of next st, K2, cast (bind) off 2 sts, K2 including st already on needle after cast (bind) off, K into front and back of next st, K3.

Row 4 K3, K into front and back of next st, P3, cast on 2 sts, P3, K into front and back of next st, K3.

Row 5 K3, K into front and back of next st, K10, K into front and back of next st, K3.

Row 6 K3, K into front and back of next st, P12, K into front and back of next st, K3. 22 sts.

Slip sts on to a spare needle.

Make a 2nd flap in the same way.

LEFT FRONT

With A and 3¾mm (US size 5) needles, cast on 52[57:62] sts.

Beg K1, P1 rib as foll:

Rib row 1 *K1, P1, rep from * to last 2[3:2] sts, K2[3:2].

Rib row 2 K2, work the rem sts by K the K sts and P the P sts.

Rep last 2 rows until 16 rows in all have been worked from beg.

Change to 4½mm (US size 7) needles and beg with a K row, work in st st foll chart between markers for left front from row 1, working incs as indicated and K2 at centre front edge on every row, until chart row 28 has been completed, so ending with a WS row. 53[58:63] sts.

Pocket

Place pocket on next row as foll:

Row 29 (RS) Inc 1 st at beg of row work 18[23:28] sts in patt, cast (bind) off next 20 sts, work last 15 sts in patt including st already on needle after cast (bind) off.

Row 30 Work in patt to cast (bound) off sts, P20 sts of pocket lining from spare needle, work rem 19[24:29] sts in patt.

Row 31 Work in patt to 1 st before pocket, holding the pocket flap with RS facing upwards work the first st of the pocket flap tog with the next st on the left-hand needle, cont in this way until all the 22 flap sts have been worked, work in patt to end of row. Cont in patt foll chart until chart row 66 is complete, so ending with a WS row. 57[62:67] sts.

Shape Sleeve

Change to 4½mm (US size 7) circular needle and working back and forth in rows and keeping patt correct throughout, shape sleeve foll chart until chart row 105 has been completed, so ending with a RS row. 121 sts.

Shape Neck

Shape neck foll chart, omitting incomplete motifs at neck edge, until chart row 132 has been completed. 106 sts.

Slip sts on to a spare needle.

RIGHT FRONT

With A and 3¾mm (US size 5) needles, cast on 52[57:62] sts.

Beg K1, P1 rib as foll:

Rib row 1 K2[3:2], *P1, K1, rep from * to end.

Rib row 2 K the K sts and P the P sts to last 2 sts, K2.

Rep last 2 rows until 16 rows in all have been worked from beg.

Complete as for left front, but foll chart between markers for right front, reversing the position of the pocket and beg the neck shaping after row 106 has been completed.

COLLAR

With A and 3¾mm (US size 5) needles, cast on 120 sts.

Work 12 rows in K1, P1 rib.

Keeping rib patt correct, cast (bind) off 6 sts at beg of next 2 rows and 4 sts at beg of next 16 rows. 44 sts.

Cast (bind) off loosely in rib.

CUFFS

With B and 4½mm (US size 7) needles and holding the RS back and left front tog, cast (bind) off both sets of sts tog to end of left front sts, cast (bind) off 30 sts of back neck, then cast (bind) off right front and back tog.

With A, 3¾mm (US size 5) needles and with RS facing, pick up and K46[48:50] sts from straight edge of end of sleeve. Work in K1, P1 rib for 16 rows.

Cast (bind) off in rib.

MAKING UP/ FINISHING

Sew side, cuff and sleeve seams. Sew down pocket linings to WS of fronts. Sew buttons to pockets. Sew in zipper to centre front. Using 7cm (2¾in) lengths of B, D and E, make a small tassel for zipper pull and attach. Sew cast (bound) off edge of collar around neckline. Press according to the instructions on the yarn label, omitting all ribbing. Fold over collar and press lightly. Keep one yarn label for washing instructions.

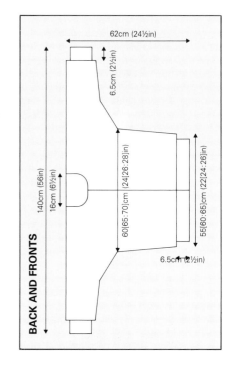

BACK AND FRONTS

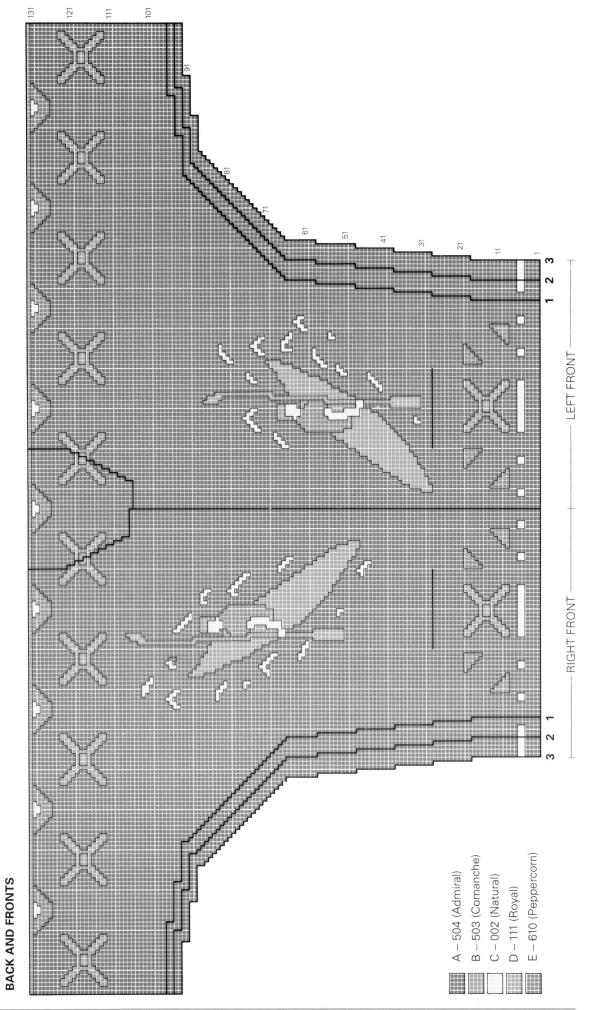

A – 504 (Admiral)
B – 503 (Comanche)
C – 002 (Natural)
D – 111 (Royal)
E – 610 (Peppercorn)

RACING

CYCLING

MATERIALS

Emu *Superwash DK*
50g (1¾oz) balls
2[2:2:3] balls No. 3088 (Green) A
3[3:3:4] balls No. 3095 (Yellow) B
2[2:2:3] balls No. 3051 (Red) C
3[3:3:4] balls No. 3079 (Cream) D
1[2:2:2] balls No. 3060 (Blue) E
3[3:4:4] balls No. 3070 (Black) F
One 18cm (7in) black zipper

NEEDLES

1 pair 4mm (US size 6) *or size to obtain
correct tension/gauge*
1 pair 3¼mm (US size 3)

TENSION/GAUGE

24 sts and 29 rows = 10cm (4in)
square measured over st st using
4mm (US size 6) needles
*Check your tension/gauge before
beginning.*

MEASUREMENTS

To fit bust:
86[91:96:102]cm (34[36:38:40]in)
Actual width across back:
46[48:51:53]cm
(18½[19½:20½:21½]in)
Length:
67cm (27in)
Sleeve length:
47cm (18½in)
*Figures for larger sizes are given
in square brackets; where
there is only one set of figures, it
applies to all sizes.*

BACK

With F and 3¼mm (US size 3) needles, cast on 110[116:122:128] sts.
Work in K1, P1 rib for 5cm (2in).
Change to 4mm (US size 6) needles and beg with a K row, work in st st foll chart for back from row 1, using a separate ball or bobbin of yarn for each area of colour and twisting yarns when changing colours to prevent holes, until chart row 180 has been completed (see chart below).
Cast (bind) off.

FRONT

Work as for back until chart row 130 is complete, so ending with a WS row.
Shape Neck
Keeping patt correct throughout, shape neck foll chart, until chart row 180 has been completed.
Cast (bind) off rem 40[43:46:49] sts (at each side of neck).

LEFT SLEEVE

With F and 3¼mm (US size 3) needles,

cast on 44[46:48:50] sts. Work in K1, P1 rib for 5cm (2in), inc 10[8:14:12] sts across last row. 54(54:62:62) sts.
Change to 4mm (US size 6) needles and beg with a K row, work in st st foll left sleeve chart from row 1 and working incs as indicated until chart row 120 has been completed. 88[88:96:96] sts.
Cast (bind) off.

RIGHT SLEEVE

Work as for left sleeve, but foll right sleeve chart.

BACK AND FRONT

4 3 2 1   1 2 3 4

NECKBAND

Join right and left shoulder seams. With F, 3¼mm (US size 3) needles and RS facing, (leaving neck opening unworked) pick up and K26 sts up right side of neck, 32 sts from back neck, and 26 sts from down left side of neck. 84 sts.
Work in K1, P1 rib for 5cm (2in).
Cast (bind) off loosely in rib.

MAKING UP/ FINISHING

Sew zipper into neck opening. Sew cast (bound) off edge of sleeves to back and front. Sew sleeve and side seams. Press according to the instructions on the yarn label, omitting ribbing, and keep one label for washing instructions.

A – 3088 (Green)
B – 3095 (Yellow)
C – 3051 (Red)
D – 3079 (Cream)
E – 3060 (Blue)
F – 3070 (Black)

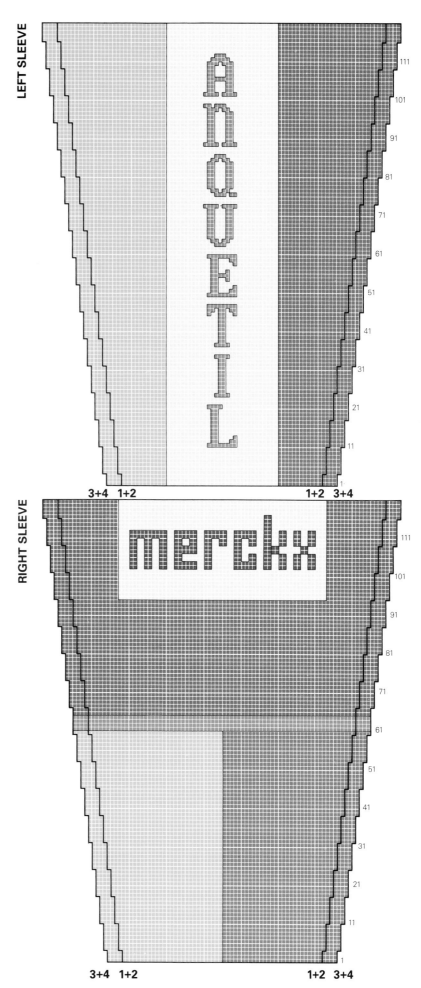

LEFT SLEEVE

RIGHT SLEEVE

3+4 1+2   1+2 3+4

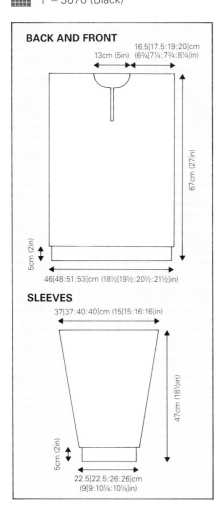

BACK AND FRONT

16.5[17.5:19:20]cm
13cm (5in) (6¾[7¼:7¾:8¼]in)

67cm (27in)

5cm (2in)

46[48:51:53]cm (18½[19½:20½:21½]in)

SLEEVES

37[37:40:40]cm (15[15:16:16]in)

47cm (18½in)

5cm (2in)

22.5[22.5:26:26]cm
(9[9:10¼:10¼]in)

MATERIALS

Pingouin *Iceberg*
50g (I¾oz) balls
9 balls No. 41 (Noir) A
4[5] balls No. 161 (Nuage) B
3 balls No. 136 (Ecru) C
4[5] balls No. 194 (Teck) D
4 balls No. 196 (Frene) E
4 balls No. 193 (Bouleau) F
5 wooden toggles

NEEDLES

1 pair 5½mm (US size 9) *or size to
obtain correct tension/gauge*
1 pair 4½mm (US size 7)

TENSION/GAUGE

14 sts and 20 rows = 10cm (4in)
square measured over st st using
5½mm (US size 9) needles
*Check your tension/gauge before
beginning.*

MEASUREMENTS

To fit bust:
92-97[102-107]cm (36-38[40-42]in)
Actual width across back:
54[60]cm (22[24]in)
Length:
78cm (31in)
Sleeve length (with cuff unfolded):
46cm (18½in)
*Figures for larger size are given
in square brackets; where
there is only one set of figures, it
applies to both sizes.*

ICE HOCKEY

HEROES

BACK

With A and 4½mm (US size 7) needles, cast on 66[76] sts.

Work in K1, P1 rib for 9cm (3½in), inc 10[8] sts evenly across last row. 76[84] sts.

Change to 5½mm (US size 9) needles and beg with a K row, work in st st foll chart for back from row 1, using a separate ball or bobbin or yarn for each area of colour and twisting yarns when changing colours to prevent holes, until chart row 138 has been completed.

With A, cast (bind) off.

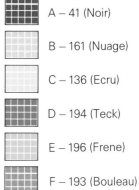

▓	A – 41 (Noir)
▒	B – 161 (Nuage)
░	C – 136 (Ecru)
▓	D – 194 (Teck)
▒	E – 196 (Frene)
▒	F – 193 (Bouleau)

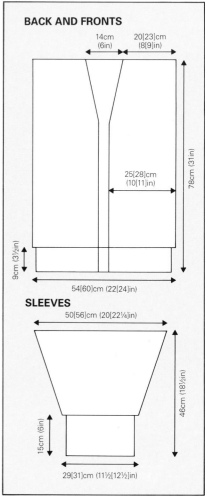

BACK AND FRONTS

14cm (6in) 20[23]cm (8[9]in)

25[28]cm (10[11]in)

78cm (31in)

9cm (3½in)

54[60]cm (22[24]in)

SLEEVES

50[56]cm (20[22¼]in)

46cm (18½in)

15cm (6in)

29[31]cm (11½[12½]in)

BACK

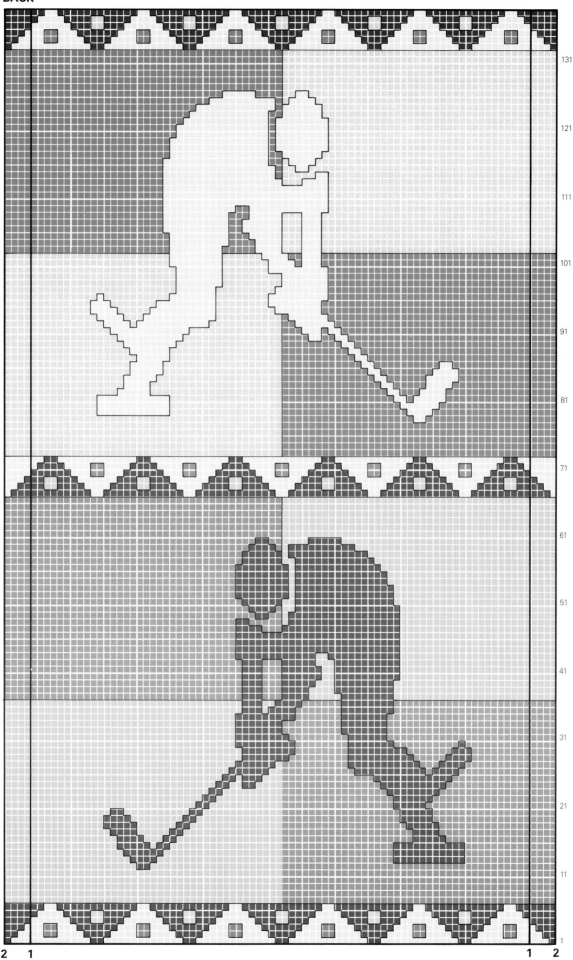

LEFT FRONT

With A and 4½mm (US size 7) needles, cast on 35[39] sts.

Work in K1, P1 for 9cm (3½in).

Change to 5½mm (US size 9) needles and beg with a K row, work in st st foll chart for left front from row 1 until chart row 90 has been completed, so ending with a WS row.

Shape Neck

Keeping patt correct, shape neck foll chart, until chart row 138 is complete. With A, cast (bind) off rem 28[32] sts.

RIGHT FRONT

Work as for left front, but foll chart for right front.

SLEEVES

With A and 4½mm (US size 7) needles, cast on 34 sts.

Work in K1, P1 rib for 15cm (6in), inc 6[10] sts evenly across last row. 40[44] sts.

Change to 5½mm (US size 9) needles and beg with a K row, work in st st foll sleeve chart from row 1 and working incs as indicated, until chart row 62 is complete. 70[78] sts. Cast (bind) off.

LEFT FRONT BAND AND COLLAR

Join shoulder seams.

With A and 4½mm (US size 7) needles, cast on 9 sts.

Work in K1, P1 rib until band, when slightly stretched, fits from lower edge of centre front to beg of neck shaping, ending at inner edge.

Keeping rib patt correct throughout, inc l st at beg of next row and at inner edge on every foll until there are 14 sts.

Work 1 row without shaping. Inc 1 st at inner edge on next row and on every foll alt row until there are 27 sts.

Work without shaping until band and collar fit to shoulder seam, ending at outer edge.

Beg dart shaping as foll:

Next 2 rows Rib to last 4 sts, turn, rib to end.

Next 2 rows Rib to last 8 sts, turn, rib to end.

Cont in this way, ribbing 4 sts less each time, until the rows 'rib to last 24 sts, turn, rib to end' have been worked.

Next row Rib across all 27 sts.

Work without shaping until collar fits to centre back neck.

Cast (bind) off in rib.

RIGHT FRONT BAND AND COLLAR

Mark the position of 5 buttons on the button band, the first 2.5cm (1in) from cast on edge, the last at beg of neck shaping with the rem 3 evenly spaced between.

Work right front band as for left front band, working buttonholes to correspond with markers as foll:

Buttonhole row 1 (RS) Rib 4, cast (bind) off 1 st, rib to end.

Buttonhole row 2 Rib to end, casting on 1 st over st cast (bound) off in last row.

Complete as for left front band and collar.

MAKING UP/ FINISHING

Sew on front bands and collar and join back seam on collar. Sew cast (bound) off edge of sleeves to back and front. Sew sleeve and side seams, turning seam half-way down the cuff, so it can be turned back. Sew on toggles. Press according to the instructions on the yarn label, omitting all ribbing, and keep one label for washing instructions.

SLEEVES

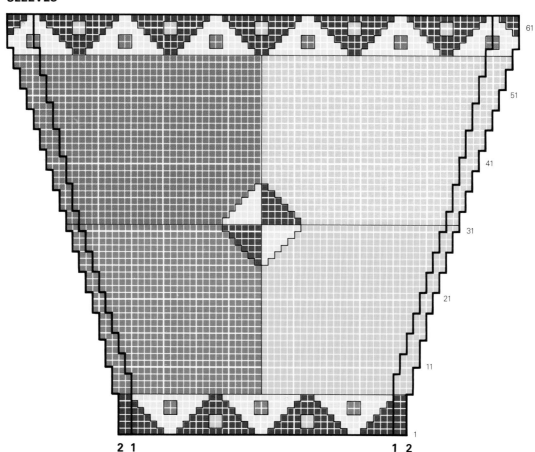

84

RIGHT FRONT

LEFT FRONT

2 1

1 2

MATERIALS

Pingouin *Mohair 50*
50g (1¾oz) balls
4 balls No. 569 (Veronese) A
2 balls No. 532 (Noir) B
2 balls No. 519 (Ecru) C
3[4] balls No. 531 (Feu) D
2 small shoulder pads

NEEDLES

1 pair 3¾mm (US size 5) *or size to
obtain correct tension/gauge*
Cable needle

TENSION/GAUGE

27 sts and 27 rows = 10cm (4in)
square measured over check patt
using 3¾mm (US size 5) needles
25 sts and 26½ rows = 10cm (4in)
square measured over zigzag patt
using 3¾mm (US size 5) needles
*Check your tension/gauge before
beginning.*

MEASUREMENTS

To fit bust:
81-86[91-96]cm (32-34[36-38]in)
Actual width across back at underarm:
50[54]cm (19¾[21¾]in)
Length:
6lcm (24¼in)
Sleeve seam:
49cm (19¼in)
*Figures for larger size are given in
square brackets; where
there is only one set cf figures,
it applies to both sizes.*

CURLING

BACK

With D and 3¾mm (US size 5) needles, cast on 124[136] sts.
Rows 1 and 2 With C, K.
Rows 3-8 With D and beg with a K row, work 6 rows in st st.
Rows 9 and 10 As rows 1 and 2.
Beg with a K row, work in st st foll chart for back from row 11, carrying colour not in use loosely across back of work and weaving it around working yarn, until chart row 50 has been completed, so ending with a WS row.
Work cable crossings on next row as foll:
Row 51 (RS) K2[0] D, *slip next 4 sts on to a cn and hold in front, K4 B, then K4 D from cn, rep from *, ending with K2[0] B.
Cont foll chart until chart row 56 is complete, so ending with a WS row.
Rows 57 and 58 With C, K.
Beg with a K row, cont in st st foll chart, using a separate ball or bobbin or yarn for each area of colour and twisting yarns when changing colours to prevent holes, until chart row 106 has been completed, so ending with a WS row.
Shape Armholes
Keeping patt correct throughout, shape armholes foll chart until chart row 166 has been completed. 84[96] sts.
Cast (bind) off.

FRONT

Work as for back until chart row 130 has been completed, so ending with a WS row.
Shape Neck
Keeping patt correct, shape neck foll chart until chart row 166 is complete.
Cast (bind) off rem 26[32] sts (at each side of neck).

SLEEVES

With C and 3¾mm (US size 5) needles, cast on 72 sts.
Rows 1 and 2 With C, K.
Rows 3-8 With D and beg with a K row, work 6 rows in st st.
Rows 9 and 10 As rows 1 and 2.
Rows 11-18 As rows 3-10.
Beg with a K row, work in st st foll sleeve chart from row 19 until chart row 24 is complete, ending with a WS row.
Work cable crossings on next row as foll:
Row 25 (RS) *Slip next 4 sts on to a cn and hold in front, K4 B, then K4 D from cn, rep from * to end.

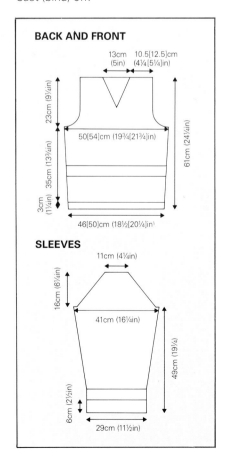

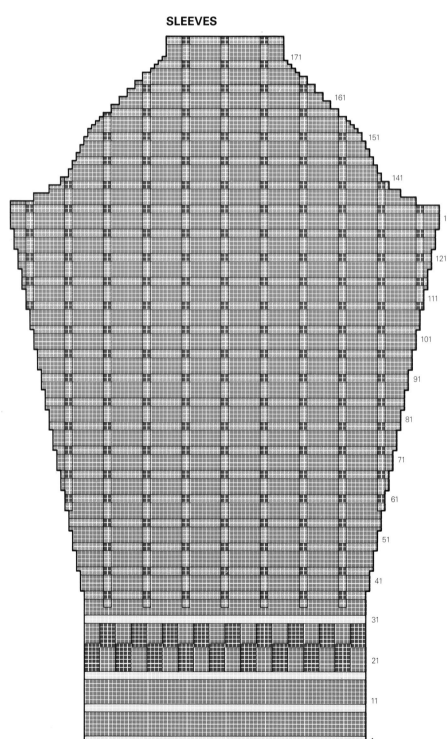

SLEEVES

Cont foll chart, working incs as indicated, until chart row 134 is complete, so ending with a WS row. 110 sts.

Shape Top of Sleeve

Keeping patt correct, shape top of sleeve foll chart until chart row 176 has been completed.

Cast (bind) off rem 30 sts in patt.

RIGHT SIDE OF COLLAR

Join right shoulder seam.

With D, 3¾mm (US size 5) needles and RS facing, pick up and K34 sts up right side of neck from centre front to shoulder seam and 18 sts to centre back neck. 52 sts.

K 20 rows (garter st). Cast (bind) off.

LEFT SIDE OF COLLAR

Join left shoulder seam.

With D, 3¾mm (US size 5) needles and RS facing, pick up and K18 sts from centre back neck to shoulder seam and 34 sts down left side of neck to centre front. 52 sts.

Complete as for right side of collar.

MAKING UP/ FINISHING

Sew sleeves into armholes, gathering at the top. Insert shoulder pads and sew down. Sew sleeve and side seams. Join back seam of collar, lap right side over left side at front and catch down. Press according to the instructions on the yarn label, and keep one label for washing instructions.

BACK AND FRONT

- A – 569 (Veronese)
- B – 532 (Noir)
- C – 519 (Ecru)
- D – 531 (Feu)

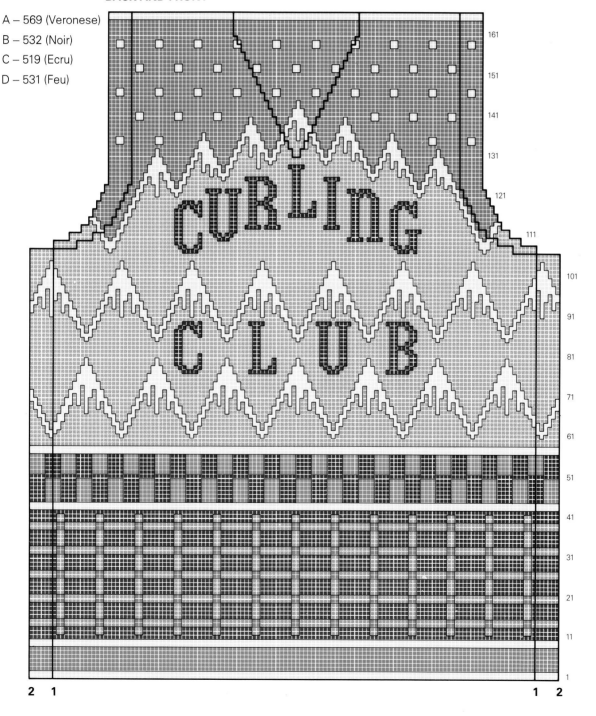

MATERIALS

Sunbeam *Aran Knit*
50g (1¾oz) balls
12[13:13] balls No. 18 (Navy) A
3[3:4] balls No. 03 (Natural) B
1 ball No. 17 (Red) C
1 ball No. 51 (Gold) D
1 ball No. 65 (Emerald) E
1 ball No. 07 (Royal) F

NEEDLES

1 pair 4½mm (US size 7) *or size to
obtain correct tension/gauge*
1 pair 3¾mm (US size 5)

TENSION/GAUGE

20 sts and 26 rows = 10cm (4in)
square measured over st st using
4½mm (US size 7) needles
*Check your tension/gauge
before beginning.*

MEASUREMENTS

To fit bust:
91[96:102]cm (36[38:40]in)
Actual width across back:
47[51:55]cm (19[20½:22]in)
Length:
59[60:61]cm (23¾[24:24¼]in)
Sleeve length:
45cm (18in)
*Figures for larger sizes are given
in square brackets; where
there is only one set of figures,
it applies to all sizes.*

SAILING

BACK

With C and 3¾mm (US size 5) needles, cast on 4 sts, then change to E and cast on 90[98:106] sts more. 94[102:110] sts. Working in K1, P1 rib, foll chart for back from row 1 for colours, using a separate ball or bobbin of yarn for each area of colour and twisting yarns when changing colours to prevent holes, until chart row 20 has been completed (see chart below).

Change to 4½mm (US size 7) needles and beg with a K row, work in st st foll chart from row 21 until chart row 154[156:160] has been completed, so ending with a WS row.

Shape Shoulders

Keeping patt correct, shape shoulders foll chart. Cast (bind) off rem 28 sts for back neck.

BACK AND FRONT

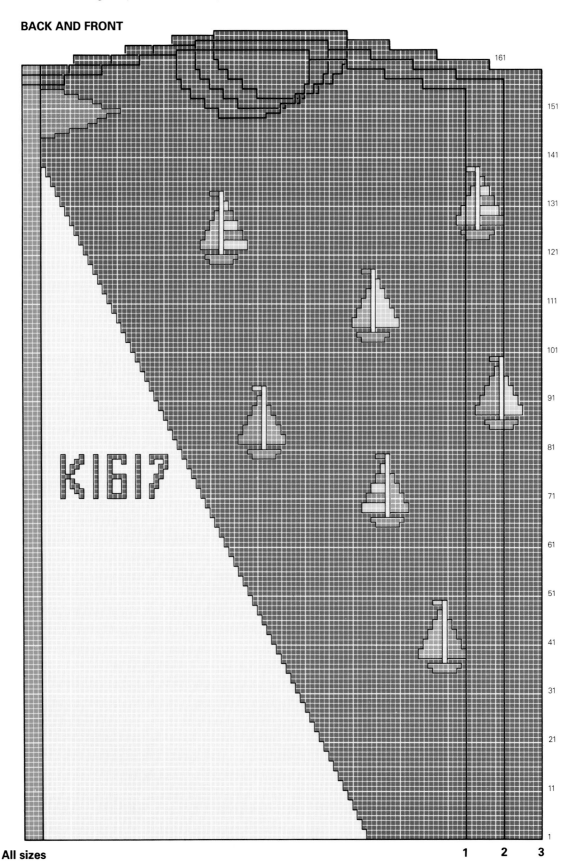

All sizes

1 **2** **3**

FRONT

Work as for back until chart row 148[150:152] has been completed, so ending with a WS row.

Shape Neck and Shoulders
Keeping patt correct, shape neck and shoulders foll chart.

SLEEVES

With E and 3¼mm (US size 5) needles, cast on 38 sts.
Change to A and work in K1, P1 rib for 7.5cm (3in), inc 8[10:12] sts evenly across last row. 46[48:50] sts.
Change to 4½mm (US size 7) needles and beg with a K row, work in st st foll chart from row 1 and working incs as indicated until chart row 98 is complete. 100[106:112] sts. Cast (bind) off.

COLLAR

With E and 3¾mm (US size 5) needles, cast on 100 sts.
Change to A and work in K1, P1 rib until

8cm (3¼in) from cast on. Cast (bind) off loosely in rib.

MAKING UP/ FINISHING

Join shoulder seams. Sew cast (bound) off edge of sleeves to back and front. Sew sleeve and side seams. Sew cast (bound) off edge of collar around neckline, from centre front to centre front. Press according to the instructions on the yarn label, omitting all ribbing. Keep one label for washing instructions.

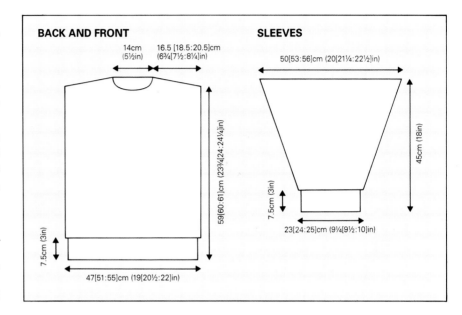

BACK AND FRONT

14cm (5½in)   16.5 [18.5:20.5]cm (6¾[7½:8¼]in)

59[60:61]cm (23¾[24:24¼]in)

7.5cm (3in)

47[51:55]cm (19[20½:22]in)

SLEEVES

50[53:56]cm (20[21¼:22½]in)

45cm (18in)

7.5cm (3in)

23[24:25]cm (9¼[9½:10]in)

SLEEVES

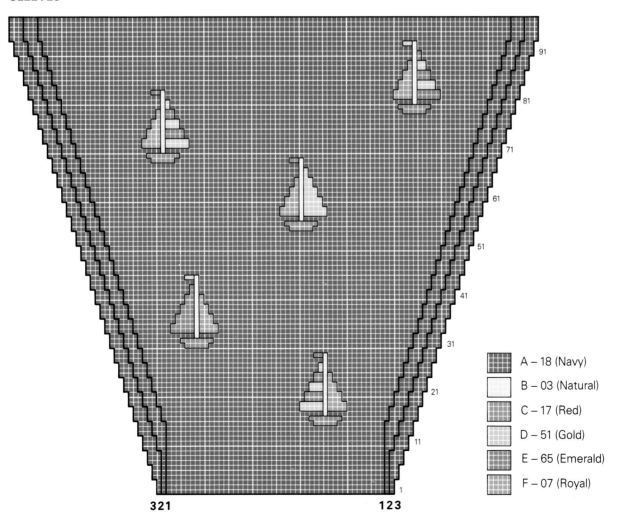

91
81
71
61
51
41
31
21
11
1

321   123

- A – 18 (Navy)
- B – 03 (Natural)
- C – 17 (Red)
- D – 51 (Gold)
- E – 65 (Emerald)
- F – 07 (Royal)

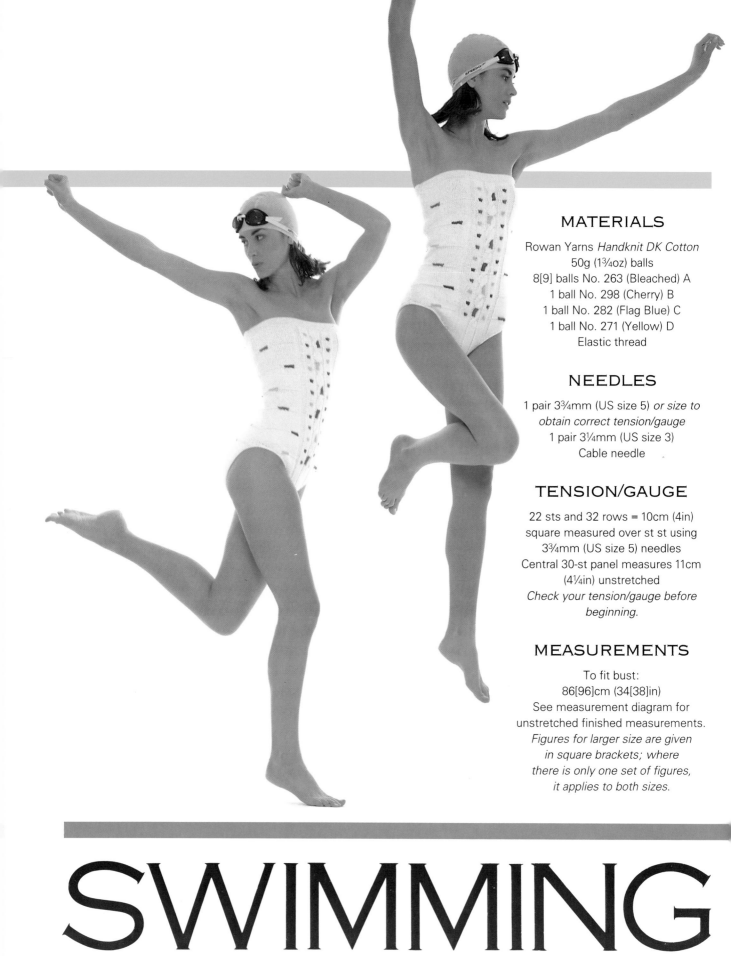

MATERIALS

Rowan Yarns *Handknit DK Cotton*
50g (1¾oz) balls
8[9] balls No. 263 (Bleached) A
1 ball No. 298 (Cherry) B
1 ball No. 282 (Flag Blue) C
1 ball No. 271 (Yellow) D
Elastic thread

NEEDLES

1 pair 3¾mm (US size 5) *or size to
obtain correct tension/gauge*
1 pair 3¼mm (US size 3)
Cable needle

TENSION/GAUGE

22 sts and 32 rows = 10cm (4in)
square measured over st st using
3¾mm (US size 5) needles
Central 30-st panel measures 11cm
(4¼in) unstretched
*Check your tension/gauge before
beginning.*

MEASUREMENTS

To fit bust:
86[96]cm (34[38]in)
See measurement diagram for
unstretched finished measurements.
*Figures for larger size are given
in square brackets; where
there is only one set of figures,
it applies to both sizes.*

SWIMMING

SPLASHES

HOW TO WORK FROM CHART

The back and front are both worked in A, except where another colour is indicated. Use separate lengths of yarn for these contrasting colours, twisting yarn when changing colours to prevent holes and stranding A loosely across back of work when not in use, weaving it around working yarn.

The chart is worked in st st (K on RS rows and P on WS rows) except where rows are marked 'knit 2 rows' (garter st) and where otherwise indicated.

Cable crossing worked on a RS row across 6 sts as foll:

Slip next 3 sts on to a cn and hold at back, K3, then K3 sts from cn.

Reverse st st worked as P on RS rows and K on WS rows.

FRONT

With A and 3¾mm (US size 5) needles, cast on 12 sts.

Row 1 K1, P2, K6, P2, K1.

Row 2 K the K sts and P the P sts.

Work foll chart for front from row 3, working incs as indicated for chosen size, until chart row 50 has been completed, so ending with a WS row. 68[76] sts.

Work next row as foll:

Row 51 (RS) With A, work into front and back of first st – called inc 1 st – K7[11] A, K6 B, K5 A, P4 A, K2 A, K2 D, K2 A, P2 A, C6 with A (see above), P2 A, K2 A, K2 B, K2 A, P4 A, K10 A, K6 D, K2[6] A, inc 1 st A.

Row 52 Inc 1 st A, K3[7] A, K6 D, K14 A, P2 A, P2 B, P2 A, K2 A, P6 A, K2 A, P2 A, P2 D, P2 A, K9 A, K6 B, K8[12] A, inc 1 st A. 72[80] sts.

Cont foll chart, working incs as indicated until chart row 62 has been completed, so ending with a WS row. 88[96] sts.

Shape Hips and Waist

Shape hips and waist foll chart until chart row 133 has been completed. 86[94] sts.

Work without shaping foll chart until chart row 170 has been completed.

Change to 3¼mm (US size 3) needles and with A, K 10 rows.

Cast (bind) off.

BACK

With A and 3¾mm (US size 5) needles, cast on 12 sts.

Work rows 1 and 2 as for front.

Work foll chart for back from gusset row 3, working incs as indicated for chosen size, until gusset row 26 has been completed, so ending with a WS row. 36[44] sts.

Cont foll chart from row 1 above gusset, working incs, colour patches, 2 knit rows and cable crossings as indicated, until chart row 62 has been completed, so ending with a WS row. 92[100] sts.

Shape Hips and Waist

Cont foll chart for *front* from row 63 (noting that there are 2 extra st st sts at each end of row on back), shaping hips and waist as indicated until chart row 133 has been completed. 90[98] sts.

Work without shaping foll chart until chart row 170 has been completed.

Change to 3¼mm (US size 3) needles and with A, K 10 rows (garter st).

Cast (bind) off.

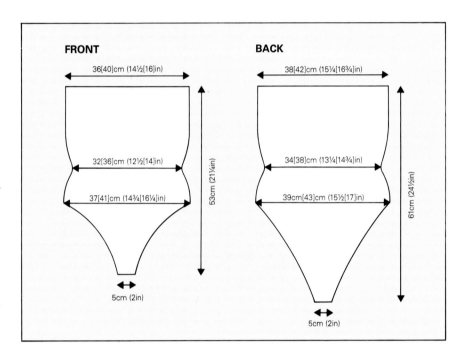

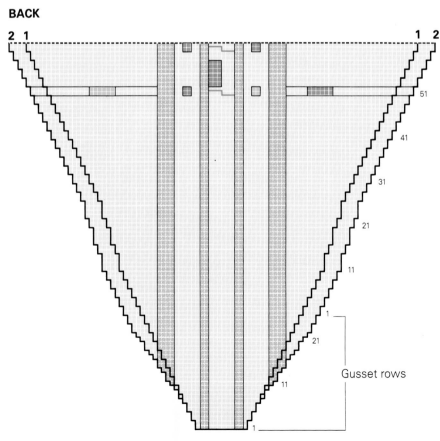

Gusset rows

STRAPS

Straps are optional and are worked as foll:

With A and 3¼mm (US size 3) needles, cast on 7 sts.

K every row (garter st) until the strap measures 48.5cm (19in) from the beginning.

Cast (bind) off.

Work a 2nd strap in the same way.

LEG BANDS

Join cast on edges of front and back at crotch.

With A, 3¼mm (US size 3) needles and RS facing, pick up and K58 sts from front along right leg opening and 68 sts from back. 126 sts.

K 1 row.

Cast (bind) off.

Work left leg to match.

MAKING UP/ FINISHING

Join side seams. With WS of garter st top facing, pass 2 strands of elastic thread through back of every 3rd st in top ridge, then again in alternate ridge down. Adjust to give snug fit and fasten ends securely. Sew on straps if desired to garter st top in suitable positions to cross comfortably at the back.

FRONT

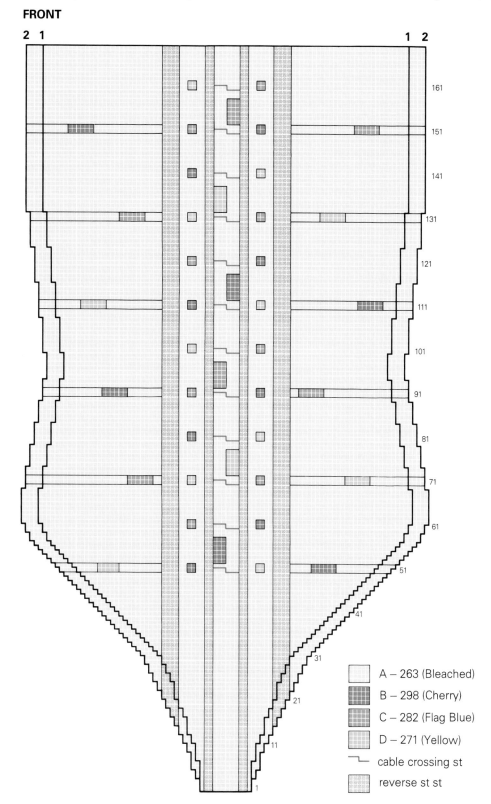

	A – 263 (Bleached)
	B – 298 (Cherry)
	C – 282 (Flag Blue)
	D – 271 (Yellow)
	cable crossing st
	reverse st st

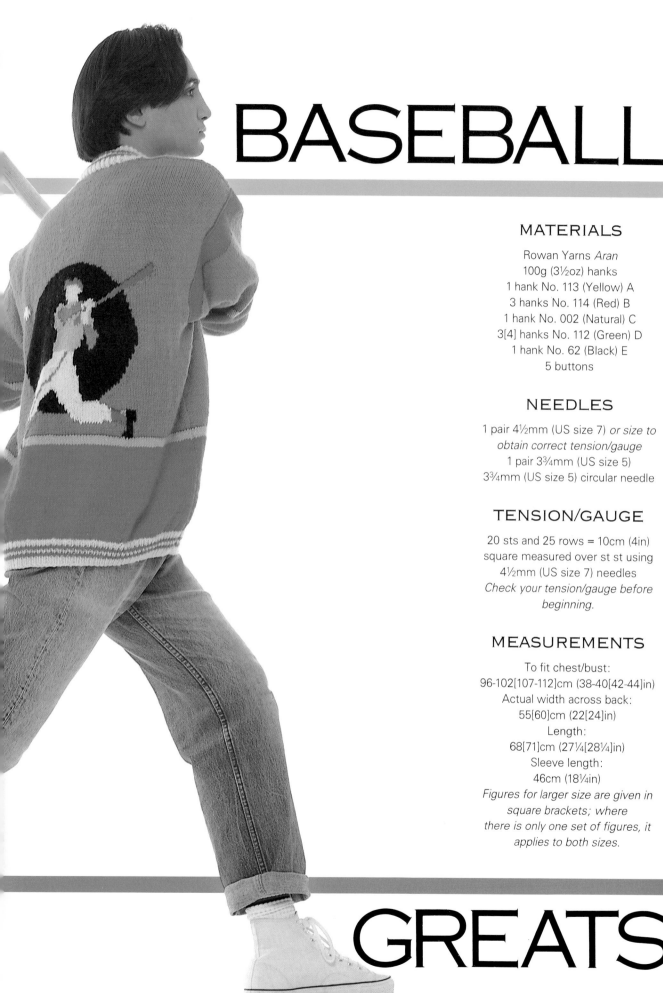

BASEBALL

MATERIALS

Rowan Yarns *Aran*
100g (3½oz) hanks
1 hank No. 113 (Yellow) A
3 hanks No. 114 (Red) B
1 hank No. 002 (Natural) C
3[4] hanks No. 112 (Green) D
1 hank No. 62 (Black) E
5 buttons

NEEDLES

1 pair 4½mm (US size 7) *or size to
obtain correct tension/gauge*
1 pair 3¾mm (US size 5)
3¾mm (US size 5) circular needle

TENSION/GAUGE

20 sts and 25 rows = 10cm (4in)
square measured over st st using
4½mm (US size 7) needles
*Check your tension/gauge before
beginning.*

MEASUREMENTS

To fit chest/bust:
96-102[107-112]cm (38-40[42-44]in)
Actual width across back:
55[60]cm (22[24]in)
Length:
68[71]cm (27¼[28¼]in)
Sleeve length:
46cm (18¼in)
*Figures for larger size are given in
square brackets; where
there is only one set of figures, it
applies to both sizes.*

GREATS

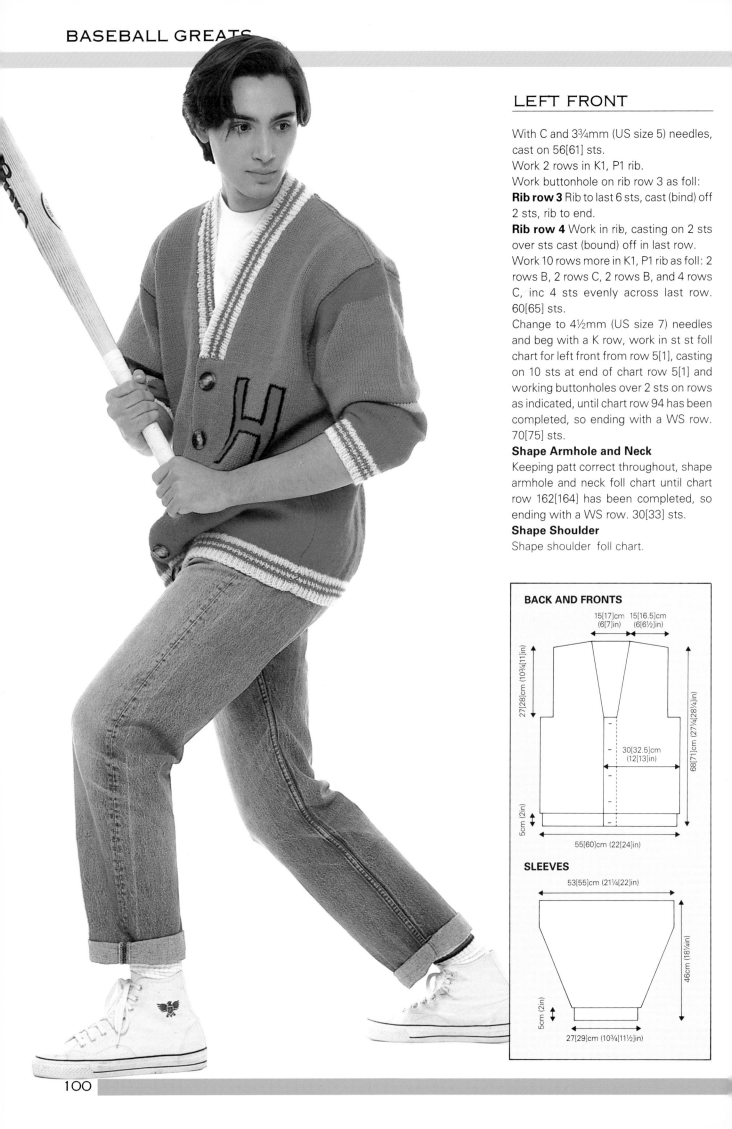

LEFT FRONT

With C and 3¾mm (US size 5) needles, cast on 56[61] sts.

Work 2 rows in K1, P1 rib.

Work buttonhole on rib row 3 as foll:

Rib row 3 Rib to last 6 sts, cast (bind) off 2 sts, rib to end.

Rib row 4 Work in rib, casting on 2 sts over sts cast (bound) off in last row.

Work 10 rows more in K1, P1 rib as foll: 2 rows B, 2 rows C, 2 rows B, and 4 rows C, inc 4 sts evenly across last row. 60[65] sts.

Change to 4½mm (US size 7) needles and beg with a K row, work in st st foll chart for left front from row 5[1], casting on 10 sts at end of chart row 5[1] and working buttonholes over 2 sts on rows as indicated, until chart row 94 has been completed, so ending with a WS row. 70[75] sts.

Shape Armhole and Neck

Keeping patt correct throughout, shape armhole and neck foll chart until chart row 162[164] has been completed, so ending with a WS row. 30[33] sts.

Shape Shoulder

Shape shoulder foll chart.

BACK AND FRONTS

15[17]cm (6[7]in) 15[16.5]cm (6[6½]in)

27[28]cm (10¾[11]in)

30[32.5]cm (12[13]in)

68[71]cm (27¼[28¼]in)

5cm (2in)

55[60]cm (22[24]in)

SLEEVES

53[55]cm (21¼[22]in)

46cm (18¼in)

5cm (2in)

27[29]cm (10¾[11½]in)

LEFT FRONT

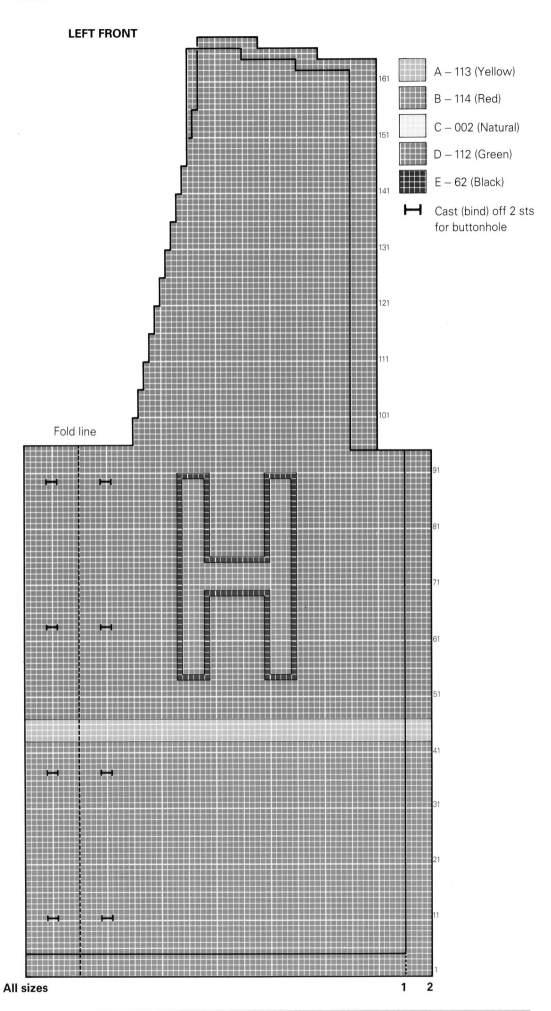

A – 113 (Yellow)

B – 114 (Red)

C – 002 (Natural)

D – 112 (Green)

E – 62 (Black)

Cast (bind) off 2 sts for buttonhole

Fold line

161

151

141

131

121

111

101

91

81

71

61

51

41

31

21

11

1

All sizes

1 2

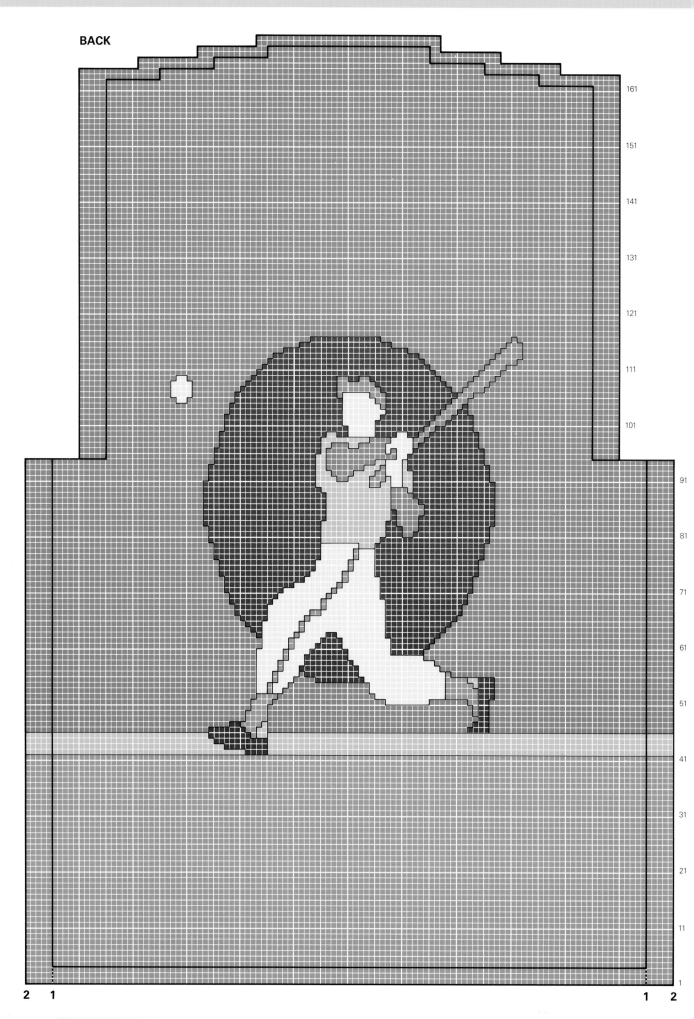

RIGHT FRONT

Work as for left front, reversing shapings and omitting 'H' motif and buttonholes.

BACK

With C and 3¾mm (US size 5) needles, cast on 100[110] sts.
*Work 14 rows in K1, P1 rib in stripes as foll:
4 rows C, **2 rows B, 2 rows C, 2 rows B, and 4 rows C***, inc 10 sts evenly across last row. 110[120] sts.
Change to 4½mm (US size 7) needles and beg with a K row, work in st st foll chart for back from row 5[1], using a separate ball or bobbin or yarn for each area of colour and twisting yarns when changing colours to prevent holes, until chart row 94 has been completed, so ending with a WS row.

Shape Armholes

Keeping patt correct throughout, shape armholes foll chart. 10 sts cast (bound) off at each side. 90[100] sts.
Cont foll chart until chart row 162[164] has been completed, so ending with a WS row.

Shape Shoulders

Shape shoulders foll chart.
Cast (bind) off rem 30[34] sts for back neck.

SLEEVES

With C and 3¾mm (US size 5) needles, cast on 40[44] sts.
Work as for back from * to ***, inc 14 sts evenly across last row. 54[58] sts.
Change to 4½mm (US size 7) needles and beg with a K row, work in st st shaping sides by inc l st at each end of 3rd and every foll 3rd row 26 times in all, AND AT THE SAME TIME work in stripes as foll:
40 rows B, 4 rows A, 34 rows D. 106[110] sts.
Work without shaping in st st with D for 12 rows and with B for 12 rows.
Cast (bind) off.

NECKBAND

Join shoulder seams.
With C, 3¾mm (US size 5) circular needle and RS facing, pick up and K64[66] sts up shaped edge of right front neck, 28[30] sts from back neck and 64[66] sts down shaped edge of left front neck, leaving cast (bound) off edge of centre front necks unworked. 156[162] sts.
Working back and forth in rows, work 13 rows in K1, P1 rib in stripes as foll:
4 rows C, 2 rows B, 2 rows C, 2 rows B and 3 rows C.
Cast (bind) off loosely in rib.

MAKING UP/ FINISHING

Fold centre front hems to WS and sew down carefully. Sew sleeves into armholes. Sew sleeve seams and side seams. Sew edge of neckband on to edge of front hem. Sew on buttons. Press according to the instructions on the yarn label, omitting all ribbing, and keep one label for washing instructions.

MATERIALS

Rowan Yarns *Designer DK*
50g (1¾oz) balls
14[15] balls No. 1 (Cream) A
1 ball No. 615 (Beige) B
1 ball No. 86 (Caramel) C
1 ball No. 616 (Brown) D
1 ball No. 89 (Light Green) E
1 ball No. 71 (Oxblood) F
Shoulder pads

NEEDLES

1 pair 4mm (US size 6) *or size to obtain
correct tension/gauge*
1 pair 3¾mm (US size 5)
1 pair 3¼mm (US size 3)
Cable needle

TENSION/GAUGE

29 sts and 32 rows = 10cm (4in)
square measured over cable patt using
4mm (US size 6) needles
27 sts and 34 rows = 10cm (4in)
square measured over combination of
patts using needles as indicated
*Check your tension/gauge before
beginning.*

MEASUREMENTS

To fit bust:
86-91[96-102]cm (34-36[38-40]in)
Actual width across back at underarm:
49[53]cm (19½[21]in)
Length:
57cm (22½in)
Sleeve length:
49cm (19½in)
*Figures for larger size are given in
square brackets; where there
is only one set of
figures, it applies to both sizes.*

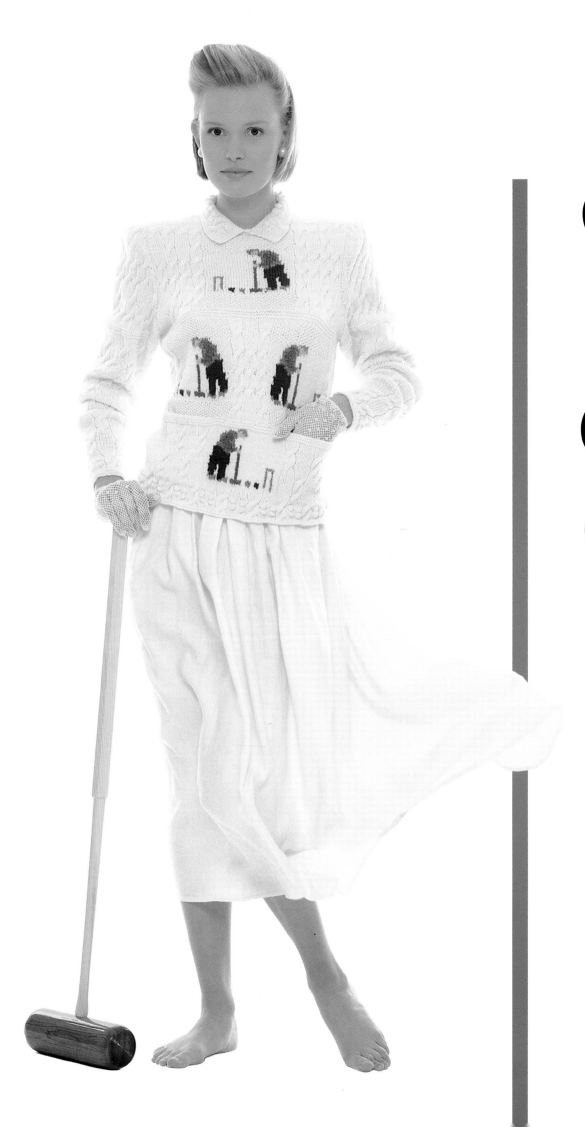

HOW TO WORK FROM CHART

Work the croquet players in st st, stranding A loosely across the back of work when not in use and weaving it around working yarn, and using separate lengths of yarn for the other colours, twisting yarns when changing colours to prevent holes.

C6 – Cable crossing worked on a RS row across 6 sts as foll:

Slip next 3 sts onto a cn and hold at back, K3, then K3 sts from cn.

On each side of 6-st cable, work 1 st in reverse st st, purling on RS and knitting on WS.

MB – Bobble worked on a RS row into 1 st as foll:

[K1, (P1, K1) twice] all into next st, turn, K5, turn, P2 tog, P3 tog, pass 2nd st on right-hand needle over first.

Moss (seed) st – Work all stitches within this outline in moss (seed) st.

St st – Work all stitches within this outline in stocking (stockinette) stitch, knitting RS rows and purling WS rows.

K every row – Rows 51-56 and rows 113-118 on back and front, and rows 85-90 and rows 147-152 on sleeves are all knit rows (garter st), worked on 3¾mm (US size 5) needles.

POCKET LININGS

With A and 4mm (US size 6) needles, cast on 29 sts.

Work 31 rows in st st, then K next 6 rows (garter st), ending with a RS row. Slip sts onto a spare needle.

FRONT

With A and 3¼mm (US size 3) needles, cast on 120[132] sts. K 2 rows.

Beg patt as foll:

Row 1 (RS) K0[6], *P1, K6, rep from *, ending last rep K0[6].

Row 2 K the K sts and P the P sts.

Rep last 2 rows once.

1st size only:

Row 5 *P1, K6, P1, C6 (see above), rep from *, ending with P1, K6, P1.

2nd size only:

Row 5 C6 (see above), *P1, K6, P1, C6, rep from * to end.

Both sizes:

Row 6 As row 2.

Row 7 K0[6], *P1, K1, MB (see above), K2, MB, K1, P1, K6, rep from *, ending last rep K0[6].

Row 8 As row 2.

Last 8 rows set position of patt.

Cont in patt foll chart for front from row 9 until chart row 18 has been completed. Change to 4mm (US size 6) needles and cont foll chart, working incs at side edges as indicated, until chart row 50 is complete, so ending with a WS row. Change to 3¾mm (US size 5) needles and K 6 rows (garter st), so ending with a WS row.

Pockets

Change to 4mm (US size 6) needles and working in patt from chart, place pockets as foll:

Row 57 (RS) Work 16[22] sts in patt, cast (bind) off 29 sts, work 34 sts in patt including st already on needle after cast (bind) off, cast (bind) off 29 sts, work in patt to end.

Row 58 Work in patt to cast (bound) off sts, *work in patt over 29 sts of pocket lining from spare needle*, work 34 sts in patt, rep from * to *, work in patt to end. Cont foll chart until chart row 120 is complete, so ending with a WS row.

Shape Armholes

Keeping patt correct throughout, shape armholes foll chart.

Cont foll chart until chart row 178 is complete, so ending with a WS row.

Shape Neck and Shoulders

Shape neck and shoulders foll chart, changing to 3¾mm (US size 5) needles after chart row 183 has been completed and working rem rows on these needles.

BACK

With A only, work as for front, but foll chart for back.

Cast (bind) off rem 36 sts in moss (seed) st for back neck.

SLEEVES

With A and 3¼mm (US size 3) needles, cast on 50[56] sts. K 2 rows.

Beg patt as foll:

Row 1 (RS) K0[3], *P1, K6, rep from *, ending last rep K0[3].

Row 2 K the K sts and P the P sts.

Rep last 2 rows once.

Last 4 rows set position of patt.

Cont in patt foll sleeve chart from row 5 until chart row 18 has been completed. Change to 4mm (US size 6) needles and cont foll sleeve chart, working incs as indicated, until chart row 154 has been completed, so ending with a WS row. 110[116] sts.

Shape Top of Sleeve

Keeping patt correct, shape top of sleeve foll chart until chart row 212 has been completed. 52[54] sts.

Cast (bind) off, while working K2 tog along row.

COLLAR

With 3¼mm (US size 3) needles, cast on 106 sts. K 2 rows.

Beg patt as foll:

Row 1 (RS) K7, *P1, K6, rep from *, ending last rep K7.

Row 2 K3, K the K sts and P the P sts to last 3 sts, K3.

Rep last 2 rows once.

Last 4 rows set position of patt.

Keeping the first and last 3 sts as K

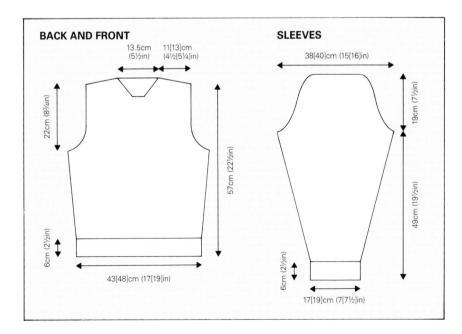

SLEEVES

A – 1 (Cream)

B – 615 (Beige)

C – 86 (Caramel)

D – 616 (Brown)

E – 89 (Light Green)

F – 71 (Oxblood)

⌐ cable crossing st

° ° bobble

knit

moss st

rev st st

all other st - stocking st

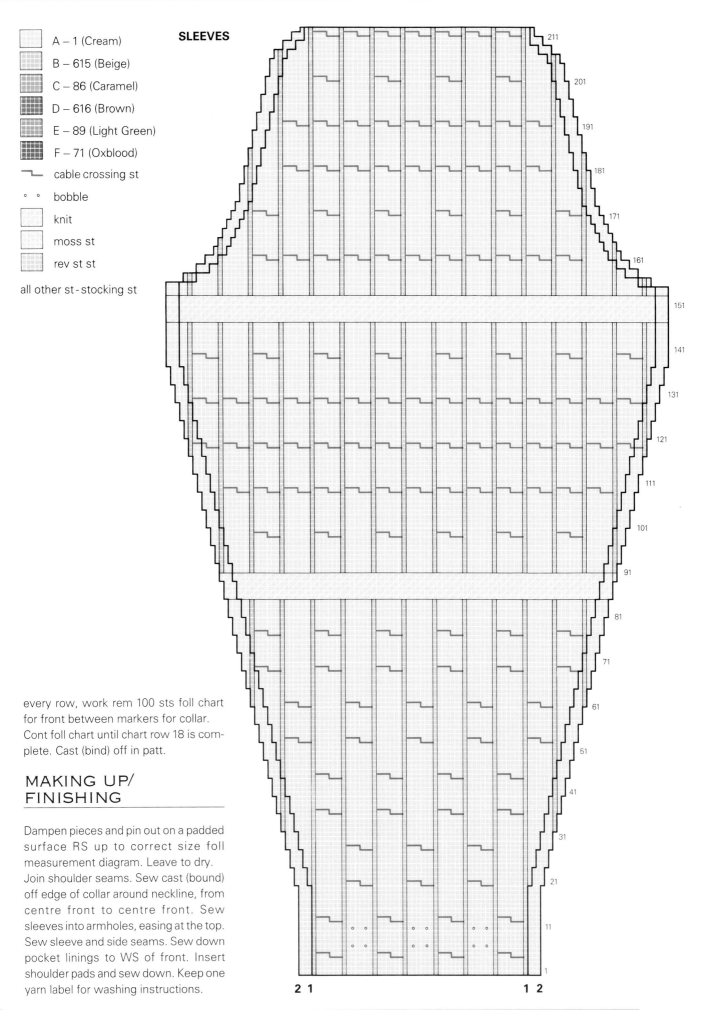

every row, work rem 100 sts foll chart for front between markers for collar. Cont foll chart until chart row 18 is complete. Cast (bind) off in patt.

MAKING UP/ FINISHING

Dampen pieces and pin out on a padded surface RS up to correct size foll measurement diagram. Leave to dry. Join shoulder seams. Sew cast (bound) off edge of collar around neckline, from centre front to centre front. Sew sleeves into armholes, easing at the top. Sew sleeve and side seams. Sew down pocket linings to WS of front. Insert shoulder pads and sew down. Keep one yarn label for washing instructions.

BACK

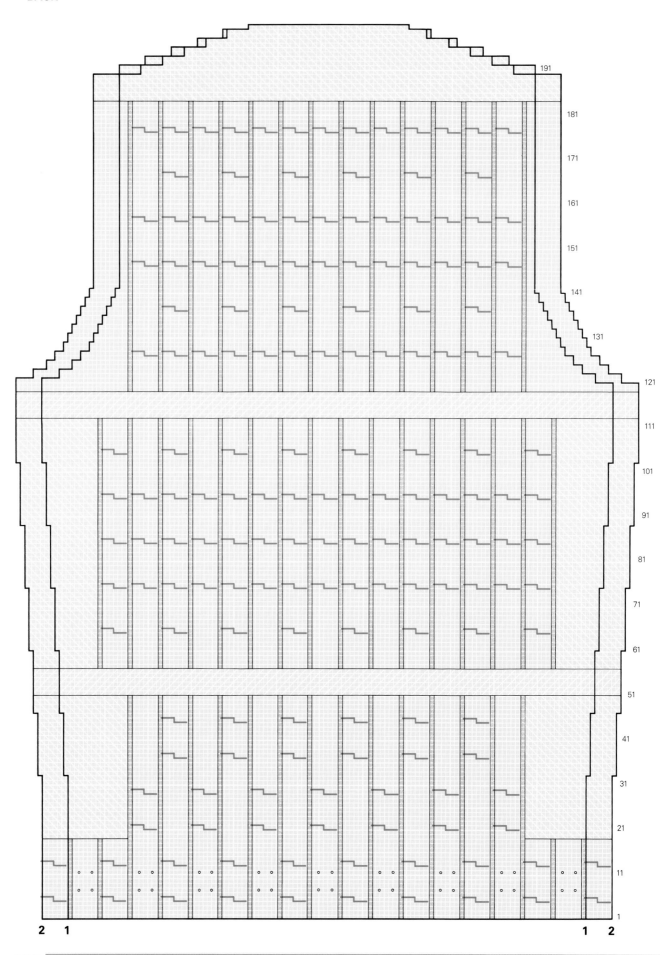

FRONT

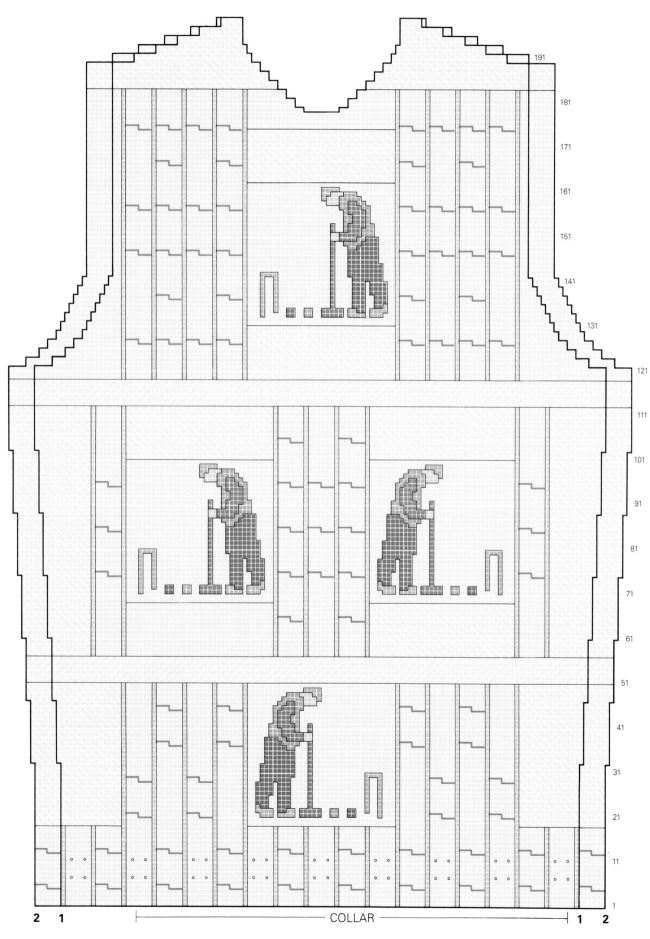

2 1 |⟵ COLLAR ⟶| 1 2

ICE SKATING

MATERIALS

Jaeger *Angora Spun*
20g (¾oz) balls
11[12] balls No. 553 (Pink) A
1 ball No. 561 (Black) B
1 ball No. 588 (Cream) C
1 ball No. 592 (Stone) D
12 small buttons
2 small shoulder pads

NEEDLES

1 pair 3¾mm (US size 3) *or size to
obtain correct tension/gauge*
1 pair 2¾mm (US size 2)
3¼mm (US size 3) circular needle

TENSION/GAUGE

28 sts and 32 rows = 10cm (4in)
square measured over st st using
3mm (US size 3) needles
*Check your tension/gauge before
beginning.*

MEASUREMENTS

To fit bust:
81-86[86-91]cm (32-34[34-36]in)
Actual width across back at underarm:
44[46]cm (17¾[18½]in)
Length (including ruffle):
54[54.5]cm (21½[21¾]in)
Sleeve seam (including ruffle):
47cm (19in)
*Figures for larger size are given
in square brackets; where
there is only one set of figures, it
applies to both sizes.*

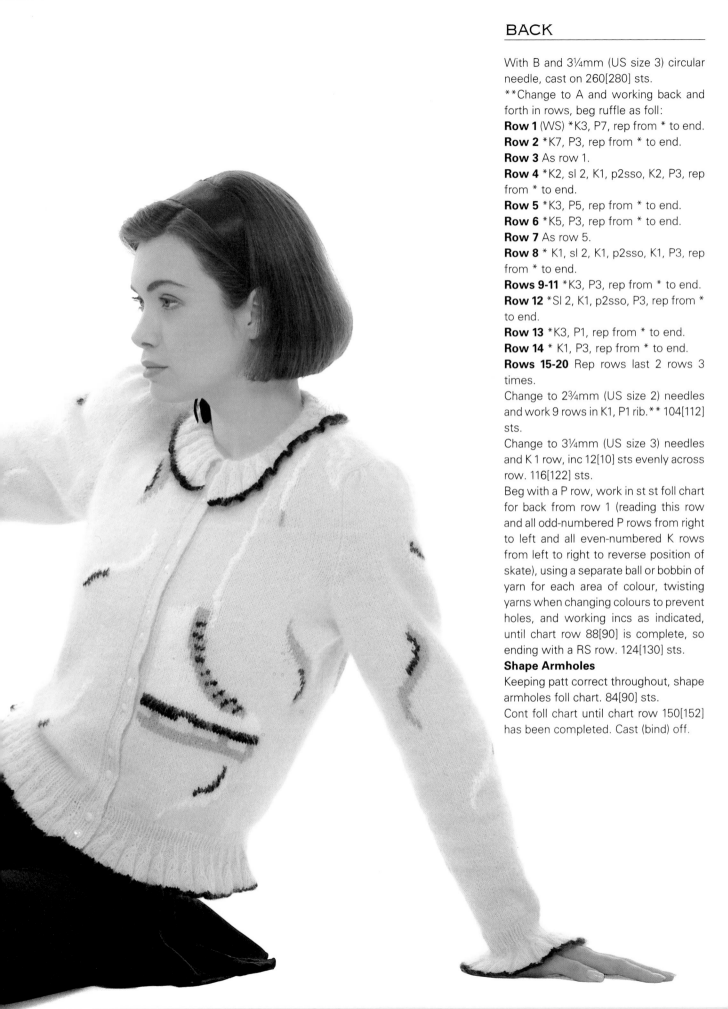

BACK

With B and 3¼mm (US size 3) circular needle, cast on 260[280] sts.
**Change to A and working back and forth in rows, beg ruffle as foll:
Row 1 (WS) *K3, P7, rep from * to end.
Row 2 *K7, P3, rep from * to end.
Row 3 As row 1.
Row 4 *K2, sl 2, K1, p2sso, K2, P3, rep from * to end.
Row 5 *K3, P5, rep from * to end.
Row 6 *K5, P3, rep from * to end.
Row 7 As row 5.
Row 8 * K1, sl 2, K1, p2sso, K1, P3, rep from * to end.
Rows 9-11 *K3, P3, rep from * to end.
Row 12 *Sl 2, K1, p2sso, P3, rep from * to end.
Row 13 *K3, P1, rep from * to end.
Row 14 * K1, P3, rep from * to end.
Rows 15-20 Rep rows last 2 rows 3 times.
Change to 2¾mm (US size 2) needles and work 9 rows in K1, P1 rib.** 104[112] sts.
Change to 3¼mm (US size 3) needles and K 1 row, inc 12[10] sts evenly across row. 116[122] sts.
Beg with a P row, work in st st foll chart for back from row 1 (reading this row and all odd-numbered P rows from right to left and all even-numbered K rows from left to right to reverse position of skate), using a separate ball or bobbin of yarn for each area of colour, twisting yarns when changing colours to prevent holes, and working incs as indicated, until chart row 88[90] is complete, so ending with a RS row. 124[130] sts.

Shape Armholes

Keeping patt correct throughout, shape armholes foll chart. 84[90] sts.
Cont foll chart until chart row 150[152] has been completed. Cast (bind) off.

BACK AND FRONTS

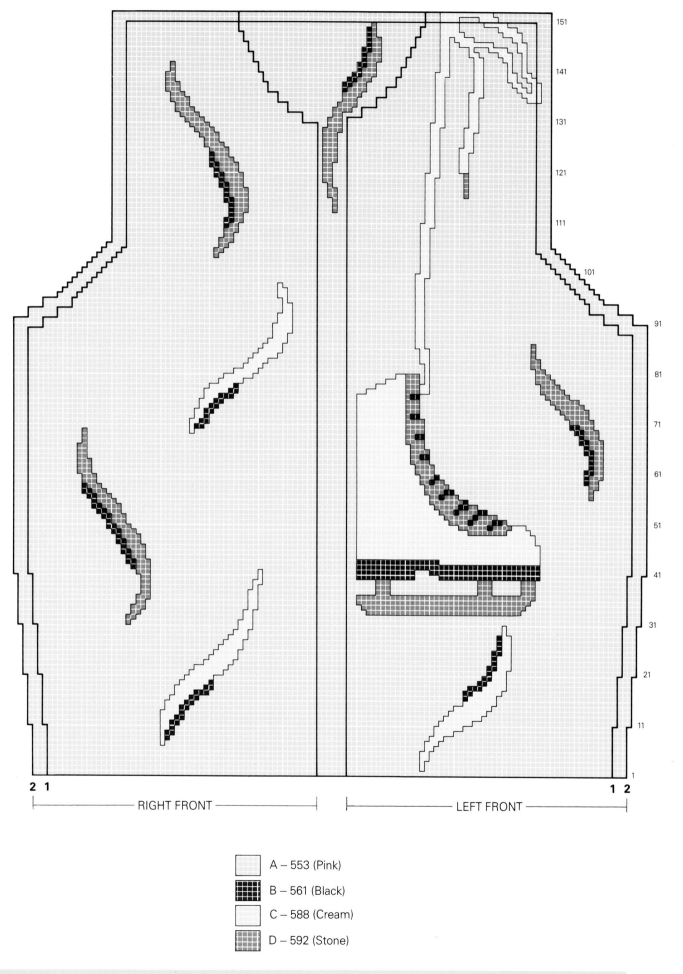

151
141
131
121
111
101
91
81
71
61
51
41
31
21
11
1

2 1
1 2

RIGHT FRONT ———————— LEFT FRONT ————————

A – 553 (Pink)

B – 561 (Black)

C – 588 (Cream)

D – 592 (Stone)

LEFT FRONT

With B and 3¼mm (US size 3) circular needle, cast on 130[140] sts.

Work as for back from ** to **, inc 3[2] sts evenly across last rib row. 55[58] sts.

Change to 3¼mm (US size 3) needles and beg with a K row, work in st st foll chart between markers for left front from row 1 (reading this row and all odd-numbered rows as K from right to left and all even-numbered P rows from left to right) and working incs as indicated, until chart row 88[90] is complete, so ending with a WS row. 59[62] sts.

Shape Armhole

Keeping patt correct throughout, shape armhole foll chart. 39[42] sts.

Cont foll chart until chart row 131 is complete, so ending with a RS row.

Shape Neck

Shape neck foll chart until chart row 150[152] has been completed.

Cast (bind) off rem 23[26] sts (at each side of neck).

RIGHT FRONT

Work as for left front, reading chart in the same way as left front but between markers for right front.

SLEEVES

With B and 3¼mm (US size 3) circular needle, cast on 130[150] sts.

Work as for back from ** to **, inc 2[0] sts evenly across last rib row. 54[60] sts.

Change to 3¼mm (US size 3) needles and beg with a K row, work in st st foll sleeve chart from row 1 (reading chart as for left front) and working incs as indicated, until chart row 130 has been completed, so ending with a WS row. 84[88] sts.

Shape Top of Sleeve

Keeping patt correct, shape top of sleeve foll chart until chart row 190 has been completed.

Cast (bind) off rem 44[46] sts.

COLLAR

With B and 3¼mm (US size 3) circular needle, cast on 277 sts.

Change to A and working back and forth in rows, beg ruffle as foll:

Row 1 P7, *K3, P7, rep from * to end.

This sets position of ruffle patt.

Cont in ruffle patt as for back until row 17 has been completed. 109 sts.

Work 2 rows in K1, P1 rib.

Cast (bind) off in rib.

BUTTON BAND

With B and 2¾mm (US size 2) needles, cast on 9 sts.

Change to A and cont in K1, P1 rib until band, when slightly stretched, fits from lower edge of centre front to neck edge. Cast (bind) off in rib.

BUTTONHOLE BAND

Mark the position of 12 buttons *in pairs* on button band as foll:

Using pins mark first buttonhole 2cm (¾in) from cast on edge and last buttonhole 2cm (¾in) below neck. Position corresponding 'pair' button at a distance of 2.5cm (1in). Space rem 8 buttons evenly between in pairs.

Work buttonhole band as for button band, working the one-stitch buttonholes to correspond with markers as foll:

Buttonhole row 1 (RS) Rib 4, cast (bind) off 1 st, rib to end.

Buttonhole row 2 Work in rib, casting on 1 st over st cast (bound) off in last row.

MAKING UP/ FINISHING

Join shoulder seams. Sew sleeves into armholes, gathering at the top. Insert shoulder pads and sew down. Sew sleeve and side seams. Sew on front bands and buttons. Sew collar around neckline, from centre front to centre front (over half of each band). Press according to instructions on the label and keep label for washing instructions.

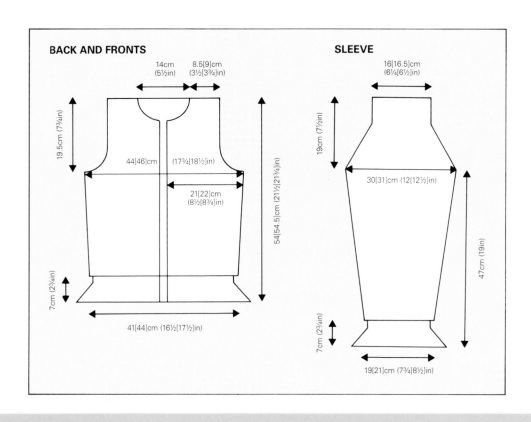

SLEEVES

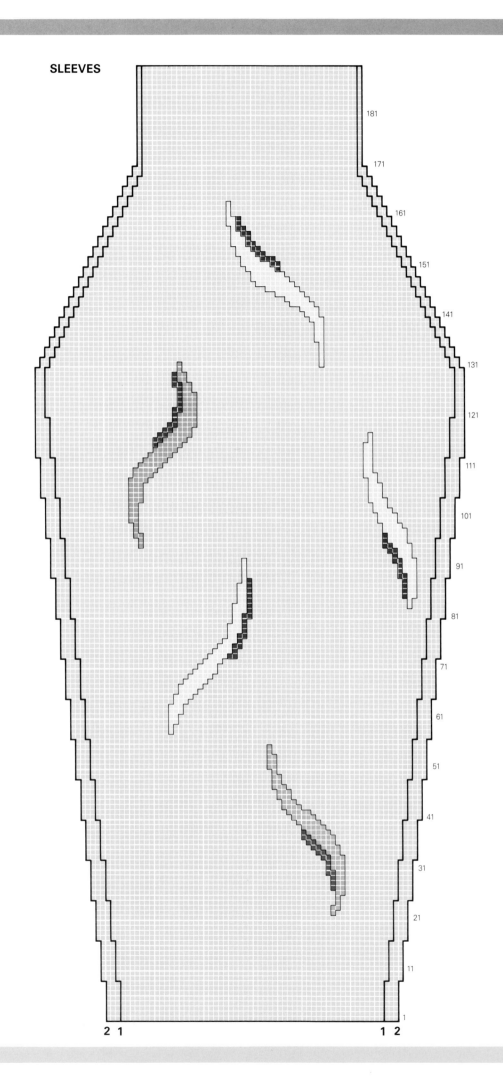

MATERIALS

Wendy *Ascot Chunky*
50g (1¾oz) balls
10 balls No. 940 (Niagara Falls) A
6 balls No. 410 (Green Spruce) B
1 ball No. 421 (Coastguard) C
1 ball No. 417 (Autumn Leaf) D
1 ball No. 399 (Aztec Gold) E
5 buttons
Shoulder pads

NEEDLES

1 pair 6½mm (US size 10½) *or size to
obtain correct tension/gauge*
1 pair 5½mm (US size 9)
Cable needle

TENSION/GAUGE

16 sts and 20 rows = 10cm (4in)
square measured over st st using
6½mm (US size 10½) needles
*Check your tension/gauge
before beginning.*

MEASUREMENTS

One size to fit up to bust:
102cm (40in)
Actual width across back:
60cm (24in)
Length:
50cm (20in)
Sleeve seam:
44cm (17¾in)

LOWER BACK SECTION

Back is worked in 3 sections, lower section, cable panel and upper section, which are sewn together after they are completed.

With B and 5½mm (US size 9) needles, cast on 96 sts.

Work 4 rows in K1, P1 rib.

Change to 6½mm (US size 10½) needles and beg with a K row, work in st st foll chart for lower band from row 1, using a separate length of yarn for each area of colour and twisting yarns when

UPPER RIGHT FRONT SECTION

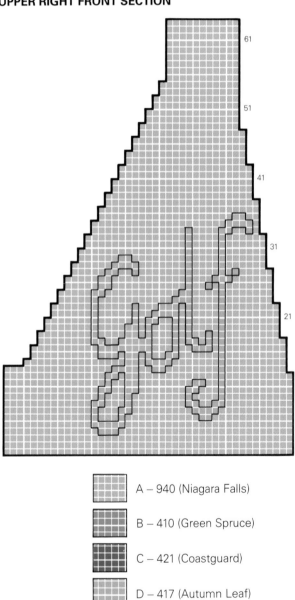

A – 940 (Niagara Falls)

B – 410 (Green Spruce)

C – 421 (Coastguard)

D – 417 (Autumn Leaf)

E – 399 (Aztec Gold)

cable crossing st

reverse st st

changing colours to prevent holes, until chart row 14 has been completed, so ending with a WS row.

With B, K 4 rows.

Cast (bind) off.

UPPER BACK SECTION

With B and 6½mm (US size 10½) needles, cast on 96 sts.

K 4 rows.

Beg with a K row, work in st st foll chart for upper back from row 1 until chart row 12 has been completed, so ending with

a WS row.

Shape Armholes

Keeping patt correct throughout, shape armholes foll chart until chart row 62 has been completed. 48 sts.

Cast (bind) off.

BACK CABLE PANEL

With B and 6½mm (US size 10½) needles, cast on 12 sts.

Beg cable panel as foll:

Row 1 (RS) K2, P2, K4, P2, K2.

Row 2 K the K sts and P the P sts.

Rows 3-10 Rep last 2 rows 4 times

more.

Row 11 K2, P2, slip next 2 sts on to a cn and hold at back, K2, then K2 sts from cn, P2, K2.

Row 12 As row 2.

Rows 13-20 As rows 3-10.

Rep rows 11-20 a total of 10 times more.

Cast (bind) off.

LOWER RIGHT FRONT SECTION

Fronts are worked in 3 sections in the same way as back.

With B and 5½mm (US size 9) needles,

UPPER BACK SECTION

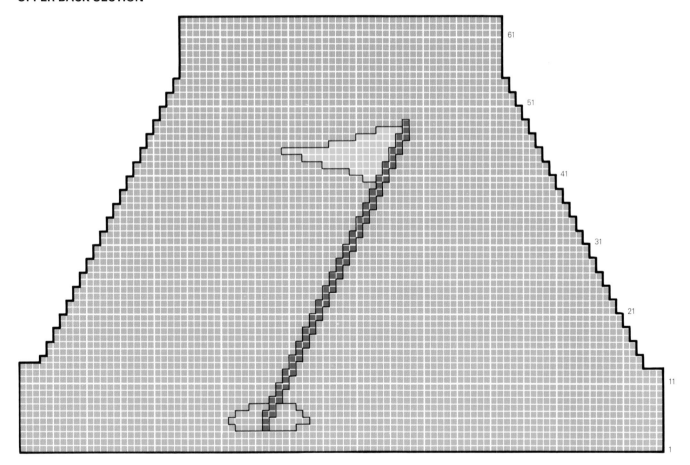

LOWER BAND FOR BACK AND FRONTS

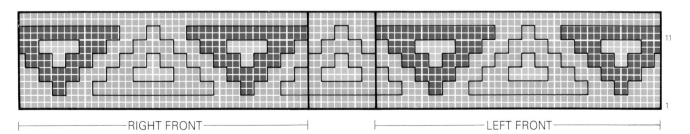

|←———RIGHT FRONT———→| |←——————LEFT FRONT——————→|

cast on 43 sts.

Work 4 rows in K1, P1 rib.

Change to 6½mm (US size 10½) needles and beg with a K row, work in st st foll chart for lower band between markers for right front from row 1 until chart row 14 has been completed, so ending with a WS row.

With B, K 4 rows.

Cast (bind) off.

UPPER RIGHT FRONT SECTION

With B and 6½mm (US size 10½) needles, cast on 43 sts.

K 4 rows.

Beg with a K row, work in st st foll chart for upper right front section from row 1 until chart row 12 has been completed, so ending with a WS row.

Shape Neck and Armhole

Keeping patt correct throughout, shape neck and armhole foll chart until chart row 62 has been completed. 11 sts.

Cast (bind) off.

LOWER LEFT FRONT SECTION

Work as for lower right front section, but foll chart for lower band between markers for left front.

UPPER LEFT FRONT SECTION

Work as for upper right front section, but reversing shaping for neck and armhole and omitting lettering.

FRONT CABLE PANELS

Work as for back cable panel to row 20.

Rep rows 11-20 of back cable panel a total of 3 times more.

Rep rows 11 and 12 once more.

Rep rows 1 and 2 twice.

Cast (bind) off.

Make another panel in the same way for 2nd front.

SLEEVES

With B and 5½mm (US size 9) needles, cast on 48 sts.

Work 4 rows in K1, P1 rib.

Change to 6½mm (US size 10½) needles and beg with a K row, work in st st foll sleeve chart from row 1 and work-ing incs as indicated, until chart row 14 has been completed, so ending with a WS row.

With B, K 4 rows foll chart until chart row 18 has been completed so ending with a WS row.

Row 19 (RS) With A, K (foll chart for incs) to centre 12 sts; with B, K2, P2, K4, P2, K2; with A, K to end (foll chart for incs).

Row 20 With A, P (foll chart for incs) to centre 12 sts; with B, K the K sts and P the P sts over centre 12 sts; with A, P to end (foll chart for incs).

Rep last 2 rows 3 times more.

Row 27 Cont foll chart, working centre 12 sts as row 11 of back cable panel. Cont foll chart, working cable panel as set and working incs as indicated, until chart row 86 has been completed. 88 sts.

Shape Top of Sleeve

Keeping patt correct, shape top of sleeve foll chart until chart row 112 has been completed.

Cast (bind) off rem 12 sts.

BUTTON BAND

Sew back cable panel to cast (bound) off edge of lower back section and to cast on edge of upper back section, taking only one half of the end K st on the cable panel into the seam and the very edge of the cast (bound) off edge of the lower back section. Sew front cable panels to the fronts in the same way, with cast (bound) off edges at centre front. Join shoulder seams.

With B and 5½mm (US size 9) needles, cast on 12 sts.

Beg rib as foll:

Row 1 (P1, K1) to end.

Row 2 K the K sts, and P the P sts.

Rep last 2 rows once more.

Row 5 (Pl, K1) 3 times, K into front and back of next st, (K1, Pl) twice, K1. 13 sts.

Row 6 As row 2.

Row 7 P1, (K1, P1) twice, K4, (P1, K1) twice.

Row 8 As row 2.

Rows 9-14 Rep last 2 rows 3 times more.

Row 15 (cable crossing) P1, (K1, P1) twice, slip next 2 sts on to a cn and hold at back, K2, then K2 sts from cn, (P1, K1) twice.

Row 16 As row 2.

Row 17 As row 7.

Row 18 As row 2.

Rows 19-24 Rep last 2 rows 3 times more.

Rows 15-24 form patt and are rep throughout.

Cont in patt until band, when slightly stretched, fits from lower edge of centre front to centre back neck.

Cast (bind) off in patt.

BUTTONHOLE BAND

With B and 5½mm (US size 9) needles, cast on 12 sts.

Beg rib as foll:

Row 1 (K1, P1) to end.

Row 2 K the K sts, and P the P sts.

Rep last 2 rows once more.

Row 5 K1, (Pl, K1) twice, K into front and back of next st, (K1, Pl) 3 times. 13 sts.

Row 6 As row 2.

Beg buttonhole on next row as foll:

Row 7 (K1, P1) twice, K2, K next 2 sts and pass first st just knit over 2nd to cast

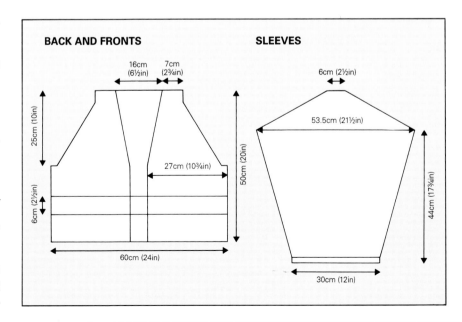

BACK AND FRONTS — SLEEVES

16cm (6½in) — 7cm (2¾in) — 6cm (2½in)

25cm (10in) — 53.5cm (21½in) — 50cm (20in)

27cm (10¾in) — 44cm (17¾in)

6cm (2½in) — 60cm (24in) — 30cm (12in)

(bind) off 1 st, (P1, K1) twice, P1.

Row 8 As row 2, casting on 1 st over st cast (bound) off in last row.

Row 9 (K1, P1) twice, K4, (P1, K1) twice, P1.

Row 10 As row 2.

Rows 11-14 Rep last 2 rows twice more.

Row 15 (cable crossing) (K1, P1) twice, slip next 2 sts on to a cn and hold at back, K2, then K2 sts from cn, (P1, K1) twice, P1.

Row 16 As row 2.

SLEEVES

Rows 17 and 18 As rows 9 and 10.
Rows 19 and 20 As rows 7 and 8.
Rows 21-24 Rep rows 9 and 10 twice more.

Rows 15-24 set patt with buttonhole. Rep these 10 rows 3 times more, then cont in patt as set, omitting buttonholes, until buttonhole band is same length as button band.

Cast (bind) off in patt.

MAKING UP/ FINISHING

Sew sleeves into armholes. Sew sleeve and side seams. Sew on front bands, being careful to match cables. Join centre back seam of bands. Sew on buttons. Press out the cable panels lightly on WS, then press the whole garment, according to instructions on yarn label. Keep one label for washing instructions. Insert shoulder pads and sew down.

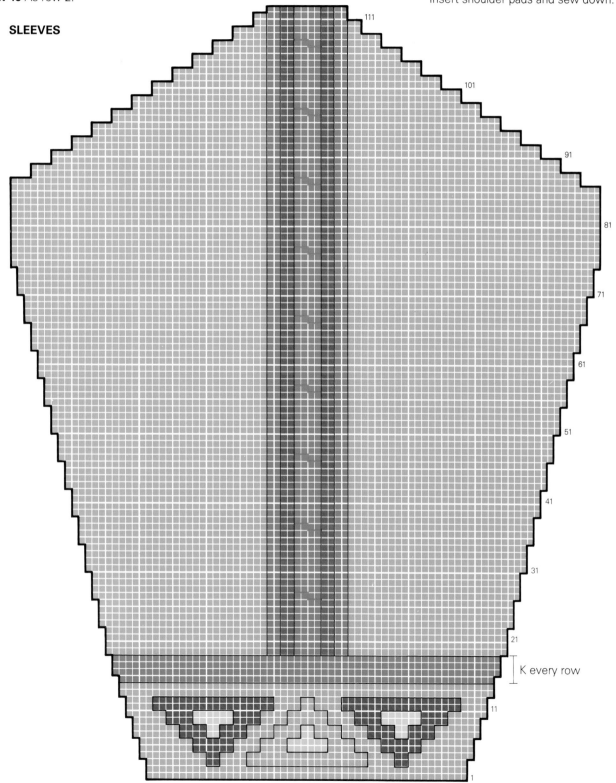

K every row

YARNS

Here are life-size photographs of the yarn used for each of the designs. Whenever possible use the yarn recommended in the pattern. If you are buying a substitute yarn, use the life-size photograph of the yarn and the general yarn weight (in parentheses) as your guideline.

POLO
Hayfield *Regal Double Knitting*
(double knitting/heavy sport yarn)

SWIMMING
Rowan Yarns *Handknit DK Cotton*
(medium-weight cotton)

AMERICAN FOOTBALL
Patons *Diploma Chunky*
(chunky/bulky)

TENNIS
Patons *Cotton Supersoft DK*
(double knitting/heavy sport yarn)

SHOOTING
Emu *Superwash DK*
(double knitting/heavy sport yarn)

SKIING
Wendy *Ascot Chunky*
(chunky/bulky)

TOURING CYCLING
Sunbeam *Pure New Wool DK*
(double knitting/heavy sport yarn)

MOTOR RACING
Sirdar *Sovereign Double Knitting*
(double knitting/heavy sport yarn)

HIKING
Hayfield *Pure Wool Classics DK*
(double knitting/heavy sport yarn)

FLYING HEROES
Rowan Yarns *Aran*
(aran/knitting worsted)

RIDING GREATS
Emu *Superwash DK*
(double knitting/heavy sport yarn)

TOBOGANNING
Jaeger *Angora Spun*
(lightweight angora)

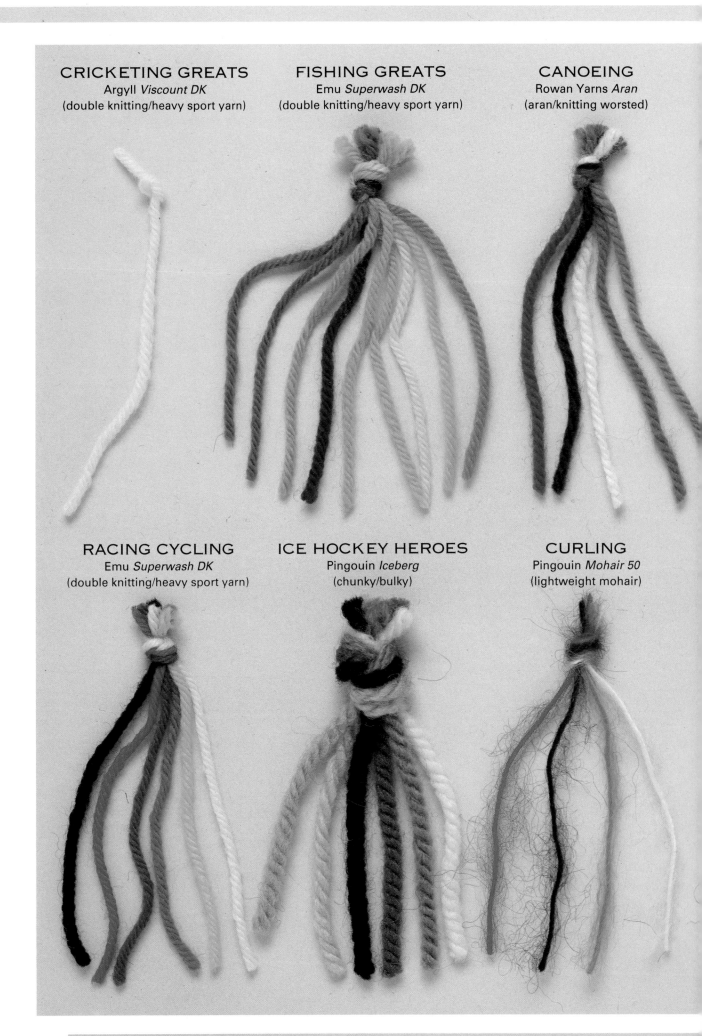

CRICKETING GREATS
Argyll *Viscount DK*
(double knitting/heavy sport yarn)

FISHING GREATS
Emu *Superwash DK*
(double knitting/heavy sport yarn)

CANOEING
Rowan Yarns *Aran*
(aran/knitting worsted)

RACING CYCLING
Emu *Superwash DK*
(double knitting/heavy sport yarn)

ICE HOCKEY HEROES
Pingouin *Iceberg*
(chunky/bulky)

CURLING
Pingouin *Mohair 50*
(lightweight mohair)

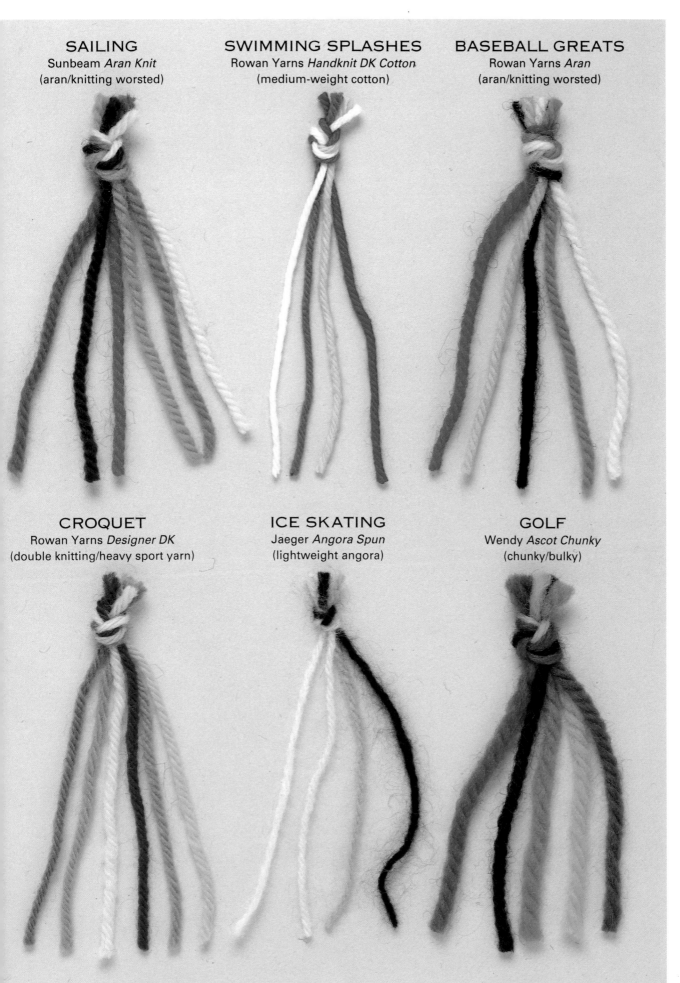

SAILING
Sunbeam *Aran Knit*
(aran/knitting worsted)

SWIMMING SPLASHES
Rowan Yarns *Handknit DK Cotton*
(medium-weight cotton)

BASEBALL GREATS
Rowan Yarns *Aran*
(aran/knitting worsted)

CROQUET
Rowan Yarns *Designer DK*
(double knitting/heavy sport yarn)

ICE SKATING
Jaeger *Angora Spun*
(lightweight angora)

GOLF
Wendy *Ascot Chunky*
(chunky/bulky)

YARN SUPPLIERS

All the yarns mentioned in the text should be readily available in the UK from good yarn suppliers. For local and international stockists, please contact the manufacturers and distributors listed below.

UK

Argyll
Argylle Wools Limited,
PO Box 15,
Priestley Mills,
Pudsey,
West Yorkshire.
LS28 9LT

Emu
Emu International Limited,
Leeds Road,
Idle,
Bradford,
West Yorkshire.
BD10 9TE

Hayfield
Hayfield Textiles Limited,
Glusburn,
Keighley,
West Yorkshire.
BD20 8QF

Patons
Patons & Baldwins Limited,
PO Box McMullen Road,
Darlington,
County Durham,
DL1 1YQ

Rowan
Rowan Yarns Limited,
Green Lane Mill,
Huddersfield,
West Yorkshire.
HD7 1RW

Sirdar
Sirdar PLC,
Flanshaw Lane,
Alverthorpe,
Wakefield,
West Yorkshire.
WF2 9ND

Sunbeam
Sunbeam Knitting Wools,
Crawshaw Mills,
Robin Lane,
Pudsey,
West Yorkshire.
LS28 7BS

Wendy
Wendy International Limited,
PO Box 3,
Guiseley,
Leeds.
LS20 9PD

USA

Argyll
Scotts Woolen Mill,
528 Jefferson Avenue,
PO Box 1204,
Bristol,
Pennsylvania 19007

Emu
The Plymouth Yarn Co. Inc.,
PO Box 28,
500 Lafayette Street,
Bristol,
PA 19007

Hayfield
Cascade Yarns Incorporated,
204 Third Avenue South,
Seattle,
WA 98104

Patons
Susan Bates Inc.,
212 Middlesex Avenue,
Chester,
Connecticut 06412

Rowan
Westminster Trading,
5 Northern Boulevard,
Amherst,
New Hampshire, 03031

Sirdar
Kendex Corporation,
PO Box 1909,
616 Fitch Avenue,
Moorpark,
California 93021

CANADA

Argylle
Estelle Designs and Sales,
38 Continental Place,
Scarborough,
Ontario,
MIR 2JA

Emu
S.R. Kertzer Limited,
105A Winges Road,
Woodbridge,
Ontario,
L4L 6C2

Hayfield
Estelle Designs and Sales Limited,
38 Continental Place,
Scarborough,
Ontario,
MIR 2T4

Patons
Patons & Baldwins (Canada) Inc.,
1001 Roselawn Avenue,
Toronto,
Ontario,
M6B 1BB

Rowan
Estelle Designs and Sales Limited,
38 Continental Place,
Scarborough,
Ontario,
MIR 2T4

Sirdar
Diamond Yarn (Canada) Corp.,
9697 St. Lawrence Boulevard,
Montreal,
P.Q.

Sunbeam
Estelle Designs and Sales Limited,
38 Continental Place,
Scarborough,
Ontario,
MIR 2JA

AUSTRALIA

Emu
Karing Vic/Tas Pty Limited,
6 Macro Court,
Rowville,
Victoria 3178

Hayfield
Panda Yarns (International) PTY Limited,
314-320 Albert Street,
West Brunswick,
Victoria 3057

Rowan
Sunspun Enterprises, PTY,
195 Canterbury Road,
Canterbury 3126

NEW ZEALAND

Emu
Karingal Vic/Tas Pty Limited,
6 Macro Court,
Rowville,
Victoria 3178

Patons
Coats Patons (New Zealand) Limited,
263, Ti Rakau Drive,
Pakuranga,
Auckland

Rowan
Creative Fashion Centre,
PO Box 45083,
Epuni Railway,
Lower Hutt

Sirdar
Alltex International,
Head Office,
Factory Road,
Mosgiel

The publishers would like to thank
Marilyn Wilson for checking the
knitting charts, and Sally Harding for
her invaluable help and advice.

The author would like to express her
grateful thanks to her knitters:
Sandra Hipperson
Jane Hipperson
Jenny Lyons
Jenny Trott
Mrs. Elliot
Jose Vale

PRINTED IN BELGIUM BY

INTERNATIONAL BOOK PRODUCTION